CLUES

W9-CBC-205

PS
1099   67-580
B5   Dahl
Z62   Robert Montgomery
          Bird   c.2

Date Due JUL   2000

WITHDRAWN

JUN 2004

JUN 09
JUL X X 2015

Date Due Date Due Date Due...

PRINTED IN U.S.A.

Twayne's United States Authors Series

Sylvia E. Bowman, *Editor*

INDIANA UNIVERSITY

Robert Montgomery Bird

ROBERT MONTGOMERY BIRD

By CURTIS DAHL

Wheaton College

Massachusetts

CUMBERLAND COUNTY COLLEGE
LIBRARY P.O. BOX 517 VINELAND N.J.

 31

Twayne Publishers, Inc.   ::   New York

PS
1099
B5
Z62

67-580
C.2

Copyright © 1963 by Twayne Publishers, Inc.

Library of Congress Catalog Card Number 62-19475

MANUFACTURED IN THE UNITED STATES OF AMERICA BY
UNITED PRINTING SERVICES, INC.
NEW HAVEN, CONN.

To the Memory of
The Reverend Professor George Dahl

Ecclesiasticus 44:1

Preface

SOME AUTHORS are important because of the high quality of their works, others because of the historical significance of what they wrote. Robert Montgomery Bird is of the second class. His works today are largely unread and, with the possible exception of *Nick of the Woods* and *Sheppard Lee*, deservedly so. The main effort, then, of this brief study of Bird is to place his literary work in the context of the literature of his time. Thus I have not tried to argue that Robert Montgomery Bird is either a great dramatist or a great novelist. Indeed, I agree with Stanley Williams that the laudable enthusiasm of Arthur Hobson Quinn and other students of the beginnings of American drama have led them to rank Bird too highly as a dramatist, for lack of someone better. Enthusiastic students of early American fiction have in the same way tended to overpraise Bird's readable and exciting *Nick of the Woods*. Yet while resisting the temptation to see Bird's real literary merits out of due proportion, I have tried to make a fair and just assessment both of his strengths and of his weaknesses. To do so, it seems to me, is to render him a truer service than to laud him for merits that he does not actually possess.

* * *

No one who writes about Bird can be anything but grateful to the biographers, editors, and scholars who have preceded him. For biographical information this book owes a great debt to Clement E. Foust's *The Life and Dramatic Works of Robert Mongomery Bird*. Without it and without Mary Mayer Bird's *Life*, edited by C. Seymour Thompson, this study could not have been written in its present form. Foust's clear reprinting of the major dramas makes the work of any scholar infinitely easier. Though I may not share all his enthusiasm, I owe much also to Arthur Hobson Quinn's meticulous research on the plays of Bird and other American dramatists of the era. No one can work in the field without referring constantly to Quinn's pioneering studies. For criticism of the novels I owe most to Alexander Cowie's *The Rise of the American Novel,* which contains by far the best extant general comment on Bird as a novelist. No student of Bird can omit reading with care and pleasure Cecil B. Williams' illuminating introduction to American Book Company's 1939 edition of *Nick of the Woods.*

In a special category I must place my acknowledgment of my constant dependence on the well-ordered collection of Bird manuscripts at the University of Pennsylvania. These provide a fascinating and almost endless storehouse of information on Bird. To the Library of the University of Pennsylvania and to Mrs. Neda M. Westlake, Curator of Rare Books, I am deeply grateful for assisting me in my examination of the collection. I wish also to express my thanks to Professor Katherine Burton of Wheaton College, who read this book in manuscript and made many valuable suggestions, and to Miss Frances Shirley of Wheaton College, who kindly read proof.

CURTIS DAHL

Wheaton College
Norton, Mass.

Contents

Contents

Chronology

1806   Robert Montgomery Bird born in New Castle, Delaware, February 5.

1810   Father dies bankrupt. Bird goes to live in home of his uncle, the Hon. Nicholas Van Dyke.

1820   Joins his mother, widowed a second time, and his brother in Philadelphia. Attends school of Mr. Pardon Davis.

1821- Attends New Castle Academy. Writes earliest sketches.
1822

1823   Attends Germantown Academy in preparation for University of Pennsylvania.

1824   Leaves Germantown Academy. Studies medicine in office of Dr. Joseph Parrish; works in druggist's shop. Enters Medical School and College of Pharmacy of the University of Pennsylvania. Is already publishing newspaper verse.

1825   Writes volume of poems, some of which are published later in *Philadelphia Monthly Magazine.*

1826   Still in Medical School. Writes early fragments of plays.

1827   Receives M.D. degree. Starts practice in Philadelphia. Finishes comedy *'Twas All for the Best* and tragedies *The Cowled Lover* and *Caridorf.* Publishes six poems and one tale in the *Philadelphia Monthly Magazine.*

1828   Gives up medical practice to embark on literary career. Writes fragmentary *King Philip, The Three Dukes,* and *Giannone.* Works on historical novel *The Volunteers,* story *Men of the Hills,* and poem *The Cave.* Publishes eight poems and two stories in *Philadelphia Monthly Magazine.* Finishes comedy *The City Looking Glass.*

1830   Completes first major tragedy, *Pelopidas,* which is accepted by Edwin Forrest.

1831   Revises *Pelopidas* for Forrest, who also offers to produce *The Gladiator*. Beginning of friendship with Forrest. *The Gladiator* opens at Park Theatre, New York (September 26). Works on poem "The Vision."

1832   Completes third major tragedy, *Oralloossa*. Publishes two poems in *New York Mirror*. *Oralloossa* opens in Philadelphia (October 10).

1833   April-September tour with Forrest to the South, West, and New England. Works on poem *The Cave;* play *The Broker of Bogota;* novel *Calavar;* and article on reviewing.

1834   Completes *The Broker* and *Calavar*. *The Broker* plays with great success in New York (February). Publishes "God Bless America" as sheet music; poem "The Beech Tree" in *New York Mirror*. Travels to England to sell *Calavar*. Unsuccessful. *Calavar* published in U.S. in October. Collects materials on conquest of Mexico for next novel *The Infidel*.

1835   Publishes seven poems and one article in *The Knickerbocker* and other periodicals. *The Infidel* published in May. Explores the Delaware Gap region, scene of *The Hawks of Hawk Hollow*. Publishes novel *The Hawks of Hawk Hollow*.

1836   Corresponds with novelist William Gilmore Simms. Publishes poem in *National Gazette*. Edgar Allan Poe asks for article for *Southern Literary Messenger*. *Sheppard Lee* (novel) published anonymously by Harper's. Elected honorary member of the Dramatic Authors Society of London following production of *The Gladiator* there.

1837   Final break with Forrest. Accepts Charles Fenno Hoffman's offer to become Philadelphia editor of the *American Monthly Magazine*. Publishes best-known novel, *Nick of the Woods*. Works on Indian story later to be called "A Belated Revenge." Publishes articles on Mammoth Cave and story "A Tale of a Snag" in the *American Monthly Magazine*. Marries Mary Mayer, June 19. Ill health forces him to relinquish editorship of *American Monthly Magazine*. Lectures at Athenian Institute, lyceum in Philadelphia.

1838   Son Frederick Mayer Bird born, June 28. Publishes *Peter Pilgrim,* collection of literary sketches. Works on last novel, *The Adventures of Robin Day.* Buys farm on Elk River below Elkton, Maryland.

1839   *Robin Day* published.

1840   Serious mental illness. Regains health through farming but loses crops in tornado and hailstorm. Leaves farm for New Castle. Becomes interested in politics through Senator John M. Clayton of Delaware.

1841   Accepts position of Professor of the Institutes of Medicine and Materia Medica at Pennsylvania Medical College, Philadelphia.

1842   Attends Whig convention in Delaware as delegate, hoping to secure nomination as Representative to Congress; fails of nomination. Publishes "Adventures in the Wrong House" in *Godey's Lady's Book.*

1843   Pennsylvania Medical College disbands. Revises dramas in hope of publication.

1846   Appointed a director of New Castle branch of Farmer's National Bank. Publishes an influential article on the Smithsonian Institution in *North American Review.*

1847   Nominated for but fails to obtain position as assistant secretary or librarian of Smithsonian Institution. Borrows money from Clayton and buys one-third interest in newspaper Philadelphia *North American.* Moves to Philadelphia.

1848   Writes an article on Yucatan and a campaign biography of Zachary Taylor. Sells farm. Has difficulties with partners in newspaper over their speculations with firm's money.

1853   Revised edition of *Nick of the Woods* published. Writes articles on Delaware Water Gap. Renewed difficulties with partners on newspaper.

1854   Dies on January 23, in Philadelphia.

CHAPTER 1

Life

DOCTOR, dramatist, novelist, historian, scientist, inventor, mechanic, farmer, politician, musician, teacher, journalist, traveler, artist—Robert Montgomery Bird was a man of fascinatingly varied talents and interests. Together with his lack of egotism, uncompromising integrity, capacity for friendship, almost quixotic sense of right, and his high concept of personal honor,[1] they make him a wholly attractive figure. He was a man respected by strangers and deeply beloved by his friends. He was trusting and unsuspicious. He had unusual abilities in a dozen different areas. Indeed, the only qualities Bird lacked were those that make for worldly success—sharpness of character and concentration of purpose. He had so many irons in the fire that he was never able to forge any single one into a weapon with which to conquer his world. His literary works in one way or another reflect all of his variegated interests.

Bird's biography is also interesting in that it reflects harshly the difficult plight of the literary man in early nineteenth-century America. If Bird turned restlessly from profession to profession, it was only partially the result of his own eager, many-sided, inquiring nature; in large part it was due to the fact that in Bird's era a man of letters in America found it very difficult to earn a satisfactory living by his pen. Bird's career was not atypical, and as an example it throws light on the careers of many hard-pressed writers of the day.

I *Youth and Medicine, 1806–27*

Even in his earliest years Bird showed the breadth of interest that was to contribute so much to his writings. Born in New Castle, Delaware, he lived first in the home of his own parents and later, after the death of his father, in that of his uncle, the Honorable Nicholas Van Dyke. His memories of his boyhood affection for his cousin Dorcas and of his cruel treatment at the hands of the schoolmaster of New Castle Academy are recorded in the early portions of his novel *The Adventures of Robin Day*. Though he was not an outstanding student—his uncle thought him idle and in need of strong discipline—he read widely in the books available to him from the New Castle Library Company. Very early he began to write verse and to acquire his lifelong interest in music.

At the age of fourteen Bird moved to Philadelphia to join his mother, by then widowed a second time, and he attended the school of a Mr. Pardon Davis, where he took lessons in drawing, an avocation which he followed with considerable skill to the end of his life. In succeeding years he was again in New Castle at the Academy, and from this period date some of his earliest stories. When he entered Germantown Academy to prepare for the University of Pennsylvania at the age of seventeen, he had the good fortune to be under the tutelage of Walter Johnson, who later was with Bird on the faculty of the Pennsylvania Medical College and who still later was chemist of the Smithsonian Institution. By him Bird was inspired to the enthusiasm for science and scientific experimentation that was one of his chief interests through life and that helped shape *Sheppard Lee* and other writings.

Though he practiced for only the briefest time, throughout his whole career Bird was spoken of as *Doctor* Bird, and his interest in medicine and in abnormal psychology is abundantly evident not only in *Nick of the Woods* and *Sheppard Lee* but in many of his other works. After his graduation from Germantown Academy he spent the summer as a student in the office of a Philadelphia physician, Dr. Joseph Parrish, and for practical experience worked in a druggist's shop. In the fall he entered the Medical School and College of Pharmacy at the University of Pennsylvania. He was awarded his degree of Doctor of Medicine in August, 1827.

Bird began the practice of medicine in an office on 13th Street near Pine Street in Philadelphia. But though he was successful as a physician and liked the purely scientific aspects of medical science, his heart was not in the profession. He was depressed by constantly seeing illness which he could not cure. Refusing to sell his humanity, he often would not charge fees and even gave away drugs free. He kept no case book. It is not surprising that he could not afford medical practice for more than a year. Thus he gave up active practice and never returned to it. Perhaps his views toward the profession are best expressed in "My Friends in the Madhouse," the first story in the book of sketches *Peter Pilgrim,* where the madman argues that the medical student is certainly mad for having entered upon a medical career, since there is more money in manual labor, since patients are ungrateful, and since quackery is more profitable and much easier.

II *Beginning of a Literary Career, 1827–30*

Bird now turned to a literary career. He is said to have published newspaper verse even as early as 1824, but it was during his years in medical school that he turned seriously to writing. He prepared a whole volume of poems, some of which were later published in periodicals. He read widely in the Greek and Roman classics, and his intense interest in Elizabethan and Jacobean drama led him to try his hand at writing plays, some fragments of which still exist among his papers. In 1827 he wrote the comedy *'Twas All for the Best* and the tragedies *The Cowled Lover* and *Caridorf;* the comedy *News of the Night* probably also belongs to this period. He also began to publish brief poems and tales in the *Philadelphia Monthly Magazine.* Six poems and one tale appeared in 1827, eight poems and two tales in 1828.

About this time Bird started what was to become a lifelong practice—the charting out in great detail of plans for future literary productions. (Great numbers of lists of projected works and of scraps with ideas for future use have been preserved among his papers.) He planned to begin as poet and dramatist, to proceed next to romance and novels, and to turn in maturer years to historical works. To prepare himself he began a wide course of reading and note-taking, including reading in a field later to become very important to him—the history and description of Spanish America. He projected at least fifty-five plays, of which he wrote fragments of at least three: *King Philip, or*

The Sagamore, The Three Dukes, and *Giannone.* He soon finished the comedy *The City Looking Glass,* and after a visit to the battlefield at Brandywine he was inspired to continue *The Volunteers,* an historical novel which he had begun on the American Revolution. Stimulated by a visit he had made to the Delaware Water Gap with his medical school friends Grimes and Black in June of 1827, he planned out his story *Men of the Hills,* which he was later to develop into the novel *The Hawks of Hawk Hollow.* The Delaware Water Gap was always to hold a peculiar fascination for Bird. Again and again he was to revisit it; its forests, streams, and glens were to be used as the background for *The Hawks;* and Bird's last literary writing was to be a series of articles describing its beauties. During this period he was also working hard on a long poem entitled "The Cave."

Such intense mental labor exacted its price. Though Bird was only twenty-three years old, his health began to suffer from prolonged application to study and writing. As relaxation he spent the summer of 1829 industriously painting pictures in New Castle, and in the autumn set out on the first of those journeys to the West that were to give him the personal background for his description of frontier life in *Nick of the Woods* and in other of his most interesting works. He traveled to Pittsburgh, then by steamboat to Cincinnati, where he spent the winter with the painter John Grimes and other friends. In late spring he returned, probably by way of Kentucky (scene of *Nick of the Woods*), to New Castle and Philadelphia. Though he returned so ill he thought he would not reach home alive, he plunged immediately into literary composition. On June 19 he began actually to write the previously sketched out story *Men of the Hills,* hoping to finish it by December 10.

III *Edwin Forrest and the Drama, 1830–34*

Though in his considerable travels through the South and West during the next four years Bird was to gather the materials on which he was later to base many of his poems and novels, his main concern from 1830 through 1834 was with drama. In 1828 the well-known actor Edwin Forrest had begun offering prizes for plays by American authors suitable for him to produce. The prize for that year had been awarded to *Metamora; or, The Last of the Wampanoags,* by John Augustus Stone, a play said by some of Bird's friends to have been filched from Bird's early dramatic attempt, *King Philip, or The Sagamore.* Bird resolved to submit a play to Forrest. By fall of 1830 he had finished *Pelopidas, or the Fall of the Polemarchs,* a play set in Thebes in 378 B.C. Forrest accepted the play and made a number of suggestions for emendations; but since there was no star part in it for him, he never produced it.

In its stead Bird wrote for Forrest a drama aimed precisely at the actor's capabilities and requirements. *The Gladiator,* which tells the story of the revolt of Roman slaves under Spartacus, was finished on May 6, 1831. Forrest immediately transferred to it the prize previously awarded to *Pelopidas* and offered to produce it either in June or in the fall. The play opened at the Park Theatre in New York on September 26 and by November 14 was playing in Boston. Its success was instantaneous. In New York, despite pouring rain, poor acting of the secondary parts, and wretchedly bad scenery and costumes, it was applauded with increasing enthusiasm each of the four nights it ran. In Philadelphia, where it was much better produced, tremendous crowds attempted to jam their way into the theater; hundreds were turned away. After the scene at the end of the second act in which the two brothers, set to fight one another in the amphitheater, recognize each other and call on the gladiators to strike for freedom, the audience rose *en masse* and cheered with a roar of applause. Bird—who in August had written in a secret diary that he had failed, that his friends had gone on to wealth and success while he had done nothing but hope, that he had no great expectations for *The Gladiator*[2]— had become a brilliant success, a popular idol inundated by flattery and patriotic praise. Had he wished, he could have become a lion of the drawing rooms.

Meanwhile Forrest and Bird had become close personal friends. They had worked harmoniously on revisions of *The Gladiator.* In June they took the first of the joint trips which were to contribute so much to Bird's knowledge of American local color. On this occasion they went first to Niagara Falls— always a favorite with Bird and the scene of one of his best short stories—and thence east to Maine and south as far as

Natural Bridge, Virginia. They returned to Philadelphia in August. The friendly partnership of dramatist and author which was to be so useful for both was in full bloom.

February, 1832, found another prize play completed, and in October it opened in Philadelphia. The theater was crowded, even though *Oralloossa, Son of the Incas* was produced in competition with the famous Kemble family playing in *Hamlet*. But though the reviews were good, the play did not wholly live up to the expectations aroused by *The Gladiator*. Nevertheless, its success was great enough to make Bird feel financially secure in his profession of playwright. As a result he rented a house and made a home for his mother in Philadelphia. His renown as a playwright also caused him to be asked to act as a judge in a short-story contest sponsored by *Godey's Lady's Book* and to contribute poems to the *New York Mirror*. Meanwhile he continued working sporadically on *Men of the Hills*.

The following spring Bird and Forrest set out on the longest and, for Bird, the most fruitful of their journeys together. They planned to go south to New Orleans and Mexico and thence, they hoped, to Peru and other countries of South America. Bird wanted to see for himself the Latin American regions whose language, archaeology, and history he had studied with such care (and which he was to use in two of his novels and one of his major plays). He planned to put even the American part of the journey to literary uses, having in mind a book of "Sketches of America" about various Southern cities. (Parts of this projected book were later incorporated into *Peter Pilgrim*.) In preparation for his Spanish American journey he obtained letters of introduction to various important men in Mexico. At the beginning of April he left New York by steamboat for Charleston, South Carolina, where he spent several days amid the excitement of the Nullification controversy. There he saw the China trees which he celebrated in a poem published two years later.

From Charleston he took the highly uncomfortable journey overland through Savannah, Augusta, Warrenton, Macon, and Columbus, Georgia, to New Orleans. Partly because of a severe epidemic of cholera in that city and partly because of a lack of funds, he and Forrest did not proceed to Mexico and South America as planned. Instead, in the middle of May, Bird traveled up the Mississippi, visiting Baton Rouge, Natchez, and Memphis, before arriving in Nashville on June 14. His friend Grimes joined him there. On their way between Nashville and Cincinnati the two friends spent four days—Bird wished it could have been two months—exploring Mammoth Cave, the subject of what was to have been Bird's poetic masterpiece. In Cincinnati he had a gay time revisiting his friends of 1831. In early July he started for Detroit and Buffalo. Having made side trips to the battle-field of River Raisin and to the grave of Tecumseh, he arrived at Niagara. After a brief return to Philadelphia, he started off immediately on a six-weeks' tour of New England. In Boston he had introductions to literary lights such as George Ticknor, Richard Henry Dana, and Washington Allston. During much of the whole tour, though unfortunately not during the time spent in New England, Bird kept a careful diary recording his obser-vations on the sights, the people, the customs, and even the lan-guage he encountered. Portions of this record he carefully worked into long travel letters to his future wife and her sister. Much of it he used in one way or another in his writings.

On his return he continued his successful career as playwright for Forrest. During the latter part of 1833 he wrote *The Broker of Bogota*, set in Santa Fé de Bogota in Spanish colonial times. The play was finished in January, 1834, and produced in February with great success in New York. "I have just left the theatre," Forrest wrote Bird on the opening night; "your tragedy was per-formed and crowned with entire success. *The Broker of Bogota* will live when our vile trunks are rotten." Yet Bird's interest in drama was beginning to wane. He was turning more and more to other literary forms. At the same time he was writing *The Broker* for Forrest, for instance, he was also working on a poem, an essay, and a novel. The poem—"The Cave"—he had begun four years earlier, but his recent visit to Mammoth Cave had inspired him to continue it. (Probably this is the same poem as that called "The Vision" on which he was working in October, 1831.) The essay, an article on reviewing originally prepared for the *United States Review*, may well have been the critique on James Mont-gomery which was later (February, 1834) placed for him in the *American Monthly Magazine* by his friend James Lawson, an active and influential literary man of New York. The novel was *Calavar; or, The Knight of the Conquest*.

IV *Novelist and Literary Man, 1834–39*

Though Bird's increasing interest in writing for periodicals was important in pointing toward his future activity as a man of letters, the really significant event of 1834 was the publication of *Calavar*. For Bird's attention was shifting more and more toward prose fiction. It is true that he had worked for a long time on the tale *Men of the Hills* and that he had published a few short stories in the *Philadelphia Monthly Magazine*. But until 1834 his primary interest had been in drama. Now he was to become a novelist, and it is as novelist that he is most widely remembered.

Much of *Calavar* had been written in the winter of 1833-34 while Bird was at work on *The Broker* also. It was finished that February and shortly afterwards accepted by Carey, Lea and Company of Philadelphia. In line with a then common practice of American publishers (Melville's publishers did as much for him), Carey, Lea held up American publication of the novel until Bird could try to sell the British rights to a publisher, since the only way for an American author to guard against the pirating of his work in Britain was to copyright and publish his work there first. Bird resolved to take his novel to England to see what he could get for it. Therefore, having collected from his friends numerous letters to prominent literary and theatrical men in England, in April he set sail for Liverpool. After visits to Chester, the Welsh mountains, Stratford-on-Avon, and Oxford, he arrived in London and was soon comfortably installed in lodgings at 3 Adam Street, Adelphi, overlooking the Thames.

However successful the tour was as a sight-seeing trip—Bird was delighted with London and enjoyed presenting his letters of introduction—as a business effort it was a failure. From Harper and Brothers he had a letter of introduction to Edward Bulwer, then a chief literary light in London. Bird took Bulwer the manuscript of *Calavar*, asking him to glance over it and give him an opinion about where it could best be published. Bulwer, at that time desperately involved in marital and financial troubles, naturally procrastinated in fulfilling the request of this American unknown until Bird, perhaps unwarrantedly, took offense and wrote a stiff letter demanding the return of the manuscript. Both from Bulwer and the British publishers, Bird learned that even if he were a British author he could expect no payment for a first novel; it would be sheer foolishness for a British publisher to pay an American author for what he could freely pirate. Like many another American author, Bird was never to earn a cent from the British publication of his books. Had the conditions of international copyright been different, he might have been able to earn a decent living as a writer of fiction, and his career as novelist might well have been different and longer.

Discouraged and ill, Bird sailed from Liverpool on his brother Tom's ship, *Carroll of Carrollton.* He arrived home without a cent and with none of the presents he had planned to bring his loved ones. Just before he had left London, he had met a fellow American about to be jailed for debt. With characteristic trusting generosity—one recalls Henry James's poignant story "Four Meetings"—Bird lent all the money he could spare to his distressed countryman. To do so, he exactly calculated every expense he would have on his homeward journey, even to the quarter for the porter who would bring up his trunk from the wharf in Philadelphia.

There now being no reason for delay, Carey and Lea published *Calavar* in October. Immediately Bird began collecting materials for a sequel, and in November, 1834, he set to work on the new novel, planning to write thirty-five pages a week and thus to end his task on the following February 13. In reality he exceeded his hopes and was finished by February 6. In May *The Infidel; or, The Fall of Mexico* was published and met a cordial reception. But Bird did not rest on these laurels. After a vacation trip in July to the Delaware Water Gap, he was inspired to turn again to the old manuscript *Men of the Hills,* which he recast into the novel *The Hawks of Hawk Hollow.* This was published in September, while Bird was on another long trip with Grimes into Kentucky and Virginia. Now a professional novelist with a rising reputation, he began to exchange books, through their mutual friend Lawson, with William Gilmore Simms, another and even better known author of Spanish American and Indian novels. He also used his rising reputation to try to help the sculptor Hiram Powers, whom he had met while Powers was proprietor of a wax-works museum in Cincinnati, obtain commissions to do portrait statues of statesmen in Washington.

The following three years saw the writing of three more

novels. In March, 1836, Harpers, to whom Bird had for some time thought of switching from Carey and Lea, accepted and published anonymously the new novel, *Sheppard Lee*. A year later appeared *Nick of the Woods; or, The Jibbenainosay*, the basic story of which Bird had heard ten years before from his Kentucky friend Dr. Black, and which at one time he had thought of working up merely as a twenty-page tale for a magazine. In April of the same year he was working on another frontier story which he himself never finished but which his son Frederick Mayer Bird completed and published as *A Belated Revenge* many years later, in 1889. Despite ill health, toward the end of 1838 Bird wrote his last novel. *The Adventures of Robin Day* was accepted by Lea and Blanchard in February, 1839, and published in April.

Though he was later to revise *Nick of the Woods* for a new edition to be published by J. S. Redfield, Bird was to write no more fiction. He abandoned his career as a novelist and turned his attention to others of his manifold interests. In part, his decision, despite the numerous plans for novels he had in manuscript, was the result of his early plans for literary life: he had determined to turn in his mature years from writing fiction to writing history. In part, the change was the result of ill health. But mostly it was caused by the simple, persistent fact that writing fiction in early nineteenth-century America simply did not pay. It is true that Bird had been unlucky: *Nick of the Woods* and *Sheppard Lee*, his two best novels, had paid him little because both had been published during a business slump. But just as he had found that he was not able to live on his earnings as a playwright, so he discovered that he could not afford to live on his earnings as a novelist. If he had had the private wealth of a Cooper, he might perhaps have continued as a professional novelist. His case is instructive in regard to the problems of other writers of fiction of his era.

Many an American author, finding that he could not live on the returns from books, had turned for subsistence to the magazines. As the careers of Edgar Allan Poe, Charles Fenno Hoffman, Cornelius Mathews, and even Nathaniel Hawthorne testify, Bird's was an age in America when the magazine, though often ephemeral individually, was tremendously important on the literary scene. During the years when Bird was writing his novels, he quite naturally also wrote for periodicals, and he hoped one day to edit his own. Indeed, his relationships with magazines, both as contributor and editor, helped to inspire and shape much of his shorter writing in both prose and poetry.

It was in 1834 and 1835 that Bird's attention turned particularly toward periodicals. As already noted, his friend James Lawson was instrumental in February, 1834, in placing a critical article by Bird in the *American Monthly Magazine*. Lawson also helped to have Bird's poem "The Beech Tree" published in the *New York Mirror* in March, though he failed in an attempt to get the *American Monthly Magazine* to accept Bird's Indian tale in verse "Colapeesa." Lawson seems to have had some hand also in the publication as sheet music in the same month of a patriotic song by Bird entitled "God Bless America." In 1835 Bird sent a political poem to the *New England Magazine* at the request of Samuel G. Howe and published several poems and an article entitled "The Community of Copyright" in *The Knickerbocker*. Anthologists were also beginning to use his work. One of his poems was printed in *The Young Man's Book* and two in *The Young Lady's Book of Elegant Poetry*. In June of 1836, Edgar Allan Poe asked him for an article for the *Southern Literary Messenger*. Bird was becoming a well-known American man of letters.

From a contributor to periodicals Bird was eager to take the step to being editor of his own magazine. Toward the end of 1836 Thomas G. Clarke, a Philadelphia publisher, proposed that a new Philadelphia literary magazine be established with Bird as chief editor. Deeply interested, Bird jotted down dozens of plans for articles. But before a final arrangement had been made, Charles Fenno Hoffman asked Bird to become the Philadelphia editor of the new *American Monthly Magazine*, which had been recently formed by joining two earlier periodicals. Hoffman, whose hope was to establish a literary magazine with national rather than sectional interests, was to be the New York editor, and Park Benjamin, the Boston editor. In the following February Bird accepted the offer, and Clarke was enlisted into the venture as Philadelphia publisher. During his brief editorship Bird published in the magazine his two articles on Mammoth Cave and his story "A Tale of a Snag." Though because of ill health he resigned from editorial duties in the fall, he was well enough in

December to be a speaker at the Athenian Institute, a lyceum at which various prominent Philadelphians gave lectures. Among his papers are the manuscripts of several lectures that he may have delivered to this audience—one, on ghosts and apparitions.

Free from his association with the *American Monthly Magazine,* in the early months of 1838, Bird resumed negotiations with Clarke for the establishment of a new magazine in Philadelphia. To be called the *Philadelphia Weekly Magazette,* it was to combine the functions of a weekly newspaper with those of a literary journal and was even to impinge on the province of the annual, since each year it was to include several plates and a number of steel engravings. Reflecting Bird's interest in music, it was to contain a piece of sheet music once a month. Bird proposed to begin the "magazette" in March with his *Peter Jones, Aeronaut,* a satirical story about a voyage to the moon. Though this whole scheme fell through, Bird had the satisfaction of being invited to contribute to the respected *North American Review.* In October, 1838, he published his collection of sketches, *Peter Pilgrim; or, A Rambler's Recollections,* much of which had been written as early as 1833 and two parts of which had already appeared in the *American Monthly Magazine.*

V *Farmer and Professor of Medicine, 1838–43*

Though Robert Montgomery Bird was probably the foremost literary man of Philadelphia, his financial future was highly uncertain, and his many interests were pulling him in divergent directions. In July of 1837 he had married Mary Mayer, with whom he had been corresponding since before 1833. In June, 1838, his son Frederick Mayer Bird, later to become a literary man in his own right, was born. Bird now had greater responsibilities than before, and he had to find a remunerative career. His first step, probably encouraged by his wife and her relatives, was to try to get Edwin Forrest to pay him the money that Bird believed was still owed him for the plays that had been so tremendously profitable to Forrest; but this move led only to a final angry rupture with Forrest and to Bird's final disgusted abandonment of any thought of making money in the theater. Nor did novel-writing offer a certain livelihood, and his labors as contributor to an editor of periodicals had netted him little. Furthermore, under the pressure of literary work (six novels, a book of sketches, and a number of short pieces in seven years) his ever precarious health was giving way.

What could a man of letters do to earn a living and regain his health? Like many another literary man, Bird dreamed that he could become a farmer and keep up his writing on the side— especially if the writing were not imaginative but historical. Early in 1838 he wrote to a friend, Samuel Groome, that he would like to buy a farm on the Eastern Shore of Maryland—he chose Maryland rather than Pennsylvania partly because, to his disgust, it seemed likely that Negroes would soon be admitted to suffrage in the latter state. Negotiations continued through the fall, and sometime that winter (in December Bird was arranging to have his land plowed), he bought the farm on the Elk River, about seven miles below Elkton, Maryland, which he was to own for at least ten years. It was a farm of 250 or 280 acres, with a beautiful view of the steamers and fishing boats on the river; but both land and house were in deplorable condition, and Bird never had enough capital or sufficiently competent tenants to have the farm put in order.

At first he evidently planned to keep the direct management of the farm in his own hands. But in March, 1839, after a draft was rejected at the bank, he was in such financial straits that he was forced to rent to a tenant. He himself had to move from Philadelphia to New Castle for a year. A year later, however, partly in an effort to regain health after a serious illness, he went to take personal charge of the farm, now called "Bird's Nest." He started with high hopes; indeed, fascinated by the theory of farming, he filled notebook after notebook with agricultural information and plans. Always a mechanical tinkerer, he sketched numerous schemes for improving plows, harrows, and other farming machines. He even invented a method of manufacturing bricks by compression, and a machine to utilize pig power. He also had a plan to get rich by mining conferra pulp (rotted river reeds) for fertilizer. None of these schemes was ever successful.

At first Bird and his wife, who joined him at the farm within a few weeks after he had moved there, wrote lyrically of farm life. Their enthusiasm, however, was dissipated by a bad hailstorm and tornado in June that utterly swept away the burgeoning crops that Bird had worked so hard to plant and cultivate. By September, 1840, he was writing that he was tired of existing as a vegetable, that he longed for Philadelphia, and that he would prefer even "life as a hack" to the vicissitudes of a farmer's existence. He missed cultured society. "For," he wrote to a friend, "after all the poeticizing on the subject of the virtues of the tillers of the soil, it is quite certain that the wicked dwellers of towns and cities make more agreeable companions and warmer friends." Moreover, like Hawthorne at Brook Farm, Bird had found that after a farmer's day, he was too tired to write, even compile, the history of America or of the United States which he had promised to Lea and Blanchard. Though from the experience he regained good health and was always to look back with great fondness on the beauty of the land itself, his experiment in farming (like most of his money-making schemes) had failed. He was forced to look elsewhere for support.

After a winter in New Castle which he probably spent working on his projected history, Bird with some reluctance turned to teaching for a livelihood, like Longfellow and Lowell and many another American author since. The Pennsylvania Medical College in Philadelphia, a branch of Pennsylvania College at Gettysburg, had been founded in 1839. On its faculty were Walter Johnson, Bird's old mentor at Germantown Academy, and Dr. George McClellan, Bird's closest medical friend. Bird accepted the position of professor of the Institutes of Medicine and Materia Medica. He was highly successful as a teacher and lecturer: twice the students paid him the honor of asking him to deliver the valedictory address, and on each occasion they requested, as they had in regard to his inaugural address, permission to publish his speech. Unfortunately, but through no fault of Bird's, the Pennsylvania Medical College disbanded in 1843; though there was vain talk of reviving it in the following year, Bird's employment there was at an end. Urging that he could continue his scientific studies and medical lectures (if the Medical College were re-established) along with teaching, his friends wanted him in 1844 to apply for the vacant post of Professor of Classical Literature in the Philadelphia high school;

but Bird refused, stating that he had no wish to involve himself in secondary school teaching.

During these years, aside from his addresses to the medical students, Bird published almost nothing—only a story (reworked from an early manuscript comedy) in *Godey's Lady's Book*. He did revise his tragedies in the hope of publishing them, and he is said to have projected a scenario tragedy with Edgar Allan Poe.[3] This last project is surprising if true, since even as early as 1840 Bird had shown that he had definitely lost interest in the theater. While he was still on his farm, his friends McClellan and Frost had negotiated in Philadelphia with the theatrical manager William E. Burton to produce *Pelopidas*, the play which Forrest long before had accepted but shelved in favor of *The Gladiator*. Burton had made two excellent offers, but Bird had rejected both. When he refused the second, his excuse was that he did not want a play of his to compete with Robert T. Conrad's *Jack Cade*.

VI *Politician and Editor, 1843–54*

Unable to support himself by literature, disillusioned with farming, and blocked in his career as professor of medicine, Bird turned to another of his many interests—politics. During his residence in New Castle he had become acquainted through Dr. McClellan with a powerful figure in Delaware politics: John M. Clayton, United States Senator (1829-36, 1845-49, 1853-56); Chief Justice of Delaware (1837-39); and Secretary of State under President Zachary Taylor. Through Clayton, Bird had become deeply and permanently involved in Whig politics. In 1842 he had been appointed a delegate to the Whig state convention. When George Brydges Rodney, the incumbent Representative in Congress, had indicated that he would decline renomination, Bird (much against his wife's more practical advice) sought the nomination. He believed that he had it safely secured; he had even written a stirring address of acceptance and planned the speeches for his campaign. But, to his mortification, Rodney decided at the last moment to accept renomination, forcing Bird to withdraw. The carefully prepared speeches were never given.

This defeat, however, had not discouraged Bird. He still hoped to find a secure, remunerative job through politics. Thus he acted as agent for Clayton at the Whig national convention of 1844 and campaigned vigorously in the election, delivering speeches all over the state. Two years later Clayton tried to reward him by getting him appointed to a prothonotary-ship in New Castle, and though that scheme failed, Bird was appointed to what was evidently a patronage job—a directorship in the New Castle branch of the Farmers' National Bank.

But the position Bird really had his eye on was not in New Castle but in Washington. Through Clayton's influence he hoped to secure the post of librarian or assistant secretary of the Smithsonian Institution. Always keenly interested in scientific and technological experimentation, Bird had filled his notebooks with records of his chemical and other experiments. He had been particularly interested, for instance, in developing a process for the cheaper manufacture of saltpeter—an interest which was the outgrowth of his fascination with caves. He had also been keenly interested in the Smithsonian Institution itself and had written a very influential article about it. Clayton did what he could to get Bird the job, but his influence was not strong enough. Though Bird was nominated, the trustees elected a man backed by even more powerful political influence.

The semi-political job that Bird did finally obtain was that of a journalist: he turned once again to earn his living by his pen. Hoping to gain financial independence, and probably at the suggestion of Clayton, he borrowed from Clayton over thirty thousand dollars and bought for twenty-six thousand dollars a one-third interest in the Philadelphia *North American and United States Gazette*. From his assumption of editorial duties in the summer of 1847 to his final illness in 1854 he poured out his energies on the paper, often working from eight in the morning till one the next morning. His partners—George R. Graham and Morton McMichael—he found of little help: they were always willing to slough off almost all the editorial work on him. Through their mismanagement and speculations the credit of the paper suffered. Indeed, because Graham had used without permission the firm's name to back his speculations, he was forced out of the company, which then became McMichael and Bird. But McMichael, too, was a weak reed who never did his share of the work; and toward the end of Bird's life a second reorganization of the firm took place. Worries about the finances of the paper and concern over his inability to repay his debt to Clayton—though Clayton generously advised him to give up the paper if the labor were injurious to his health—hastened Bird's death.

Bird was a good newspaper editor. Under his aegis the *North American* became exceedingly influential. Though the paper was Whig, it often took an independent line; and though Clayton stood behind it financially and indeed often sent articles to Bird for inclusion in it, neither he nor Bird wished his connection with the publication known. Bird's editorials, vigorous and well written, had high literary quality. That in their own time they did not seem so strong as those of some other editors is due to the fact that Bird refused to be vituperative. Bird's main contribution to American journalism, it has been said, was the well-written and readable paragraph.[4]

Bird's incessant work on the *North American* left him almost no time for other activities, and a great deal of the time he was not in good health. Occasionally he went down to Clayton's estate "Buena Vista" for a holiday of a day or two. He wrote a biography of General Zachary Taylor for the campaign of 1848. A year later, still hoping for a government job, he went to Washington with Clayton and had an interview with the President. In 1851 he contemplated a suit against Forrest for the money he felt was owed him, and in 1852 he cooperated with Boker in promoting a dramatic copyright bill. In the same year he planned a trip to the South and West in hope of regaining his health, and in 1853 he was at the "Kittatiny House" in his beloved Delaware Water Gap, from which he sent several descriptive papers to the *North American*. Business worries increased. Late in 1853 he fell ill and was confined to his home. His case became serious in January, 1854, and on January 23, at the early age of forty-eight, Bird died of "effusion of the brain." He was buried in Laurel Hill Cemetery in Philadelphia.[5]

CHAPTER 2

Poetry

A LTHOUGH Robert Montgomery Bird was known to his contemporaries primarily as dramatist and novelist, his first appearance in print was as a poet, and he turned to poetry for relaxation and pleasure throughout his whole life. He began his poetical career early. At about the age of twelve or thirteen he wrote a grand long epical poem which his cousin stole from its hiding place and, to Bird's mortification, read to the assembled family with mighty flourishes. At the age of seventeen he may possibly even have had some poems printed for private distribution. In the warm months of 1825 (when he was nineteen) he prepared a whole volume of poetry. Though he burned most of this early work, some has survived in a manuscript collection of twelve poems entitled "Juvenile Poems."

From other eras of his poetic career a great mass of manuscript poems and fragments has survived. Notebook after notebook, many of them evidently prepared for press, gives testimony to his poetic facility. Some of the earlier of these poems are translations. Others, probably dating from 1832 and the following years, are fragments of the several volumes of verse which Bird projected. He planned, for instance, a volume to be called *The Alleghenies and Other Poems.* Another plan was for a series of poems on Spanish America to be entitled *El Dorado.* A third plan, brought to completion or near completion in manuscript, was for a volume of sonnets. To prepare himself to write these, of which there are several manuscript volumes written on tastefully colored paper, Bird learned Italian and studied Petrarch. Unfortunately, the sonnets are loose, wordy, and sentimental.

In general, Bird's poetry is not of high distinction. Although in his own time it was praised for its "great delicacy, simplicity, and sweetness" and was fairly widely anthologized, it is of greater value now as exemplifying the taste of the time than for any intrinsic poetic merit.

I *Poems in* Philadelphia Monthly Magazine

Bird's first considerable vehicle for publication of his poetry was the *Philadelphia Monthly Magazine* published by his friend Doctor Snowden. In 1827 and 1828 he published twelve poems in this magazine, all but one while the magazine was still in Snowden's hands. Two of the poems are translations from Horace. That from the Bandusian ode is insipid, but the other (Book IV, Ode xiii) contains such spirited stanzas as:

> The Gods have heard, at last have heard my prayer—
> I see my Lyce rather worse for wear:
> Yet still, though old and wrinkled, she'll assume
> A girl's deportment and a beauty's bloom;
> And as she dips her thin lips in the bowl,
> Call Cupid down to satisfy her soul!

and

> And thou wert spared! For what? I hardly know:
> To shame the raven with thy locks of snow!
> To see thy lamp of loveliness decay,
> Thyself the ashes scattered on the way;
> While all thy lovers to the ruins haste,
> And laugh, like me, that it is quenched at last![1]

Three are songs. "Rest in Thine Isle, Young Hero, Rest" is about a young American officer buried in the lovely bowers of an uninhabited island of the Pacific. We shall grieve for him, Bird writes, but his memory will be forever entwined with the beauty of the isle in which he rests. "Changing Heart Away from Me" is a conventional song about a woman who has been false to her lover but who later will regret her fickleness. In "The Love-Sick Minstrel" the poor minstrel, deeply in love with a lady too high and great for him, grieves while he must pretend to be joyous. He can gain his lady's smiles only by singing of others' love for her. Of the other poems, "The Dying Bride" is a poem of sentimental melancholy about the last kiss of a bride expiring in her bridegroom's arms; "Friendship" tritely observes that, though not so intense as love, friendship lasts longer; "Brunette" plays on the Shakespearean motif of the dark woman; and the "Miniature" tells of a lover who cannot drive out of his heart the memory of his love for his sweetheart, even though she has "fallen" and is therefore now lost to him. Though woman falls and man ages, the miniature portrait remains lovely.

Far more vigorous are the more dramatic or melodramatic poems "The Death of Meleager" and "Saul's Last Day." In the former Bird tells, in alternating stanzas, of Althea piling on the faggots and of Meleager's death. The latter, which reminds one a little of Browning as the former does of Swinburne, gives in heroic couplets a highly colored account of Saul, who, in the fury of a fit of madness, prophesies his fall and refuses to postpone his death. The poem has some striking description:

> That day the spirit of the monarch fled,
> His hand was nerveless, and his heart was dead:
> Around him thousands in their armour stood,
> And, marvelling, watched their gloomy leader's mood.
> On his strong limbs the jointed brass was hung,
> The tempered falchion on his harness rung;
> Strapped to his arm, the plaited buckler shone,
> And spear and jav'lin at his feet were thrown.
> From his dark front the frowning plume descends,
> On his brow waves, and o'er his shoulder bends;
> And such a brow! While all around, elate
> With triumph shone, or wrinkled black with hate,
> His, his alone of all the martial crew,
> Retained a ghastly and a craven hue.

Horror descends on Saul's soul, and he no longer has David to calm him with his lyre. In the battle that rages his forces are defeated; his companions urge him to flee, but he refuses:

> "Back, back, great king! Gilboa's caves shall show
> Some present refuge from the unsparing foe."
> "Said I not thus?" the desperate chief replied,
> The winged arrow trembling in his side:
> "Said I not thus, the godless should prevail
> And Israel fall, like corn before the hail?
> Where are my sons?"—"These corses!"—"Said I not—
> A monarch's children like a beggar's rot. . . . "

In the conclusion he asks for death, and one of his servants kills him:

> He said: the weapon made its furious way—
> And night and horror closed the fatal day.[2]

The last poem by Bird in the *Philadelphia Monthly Magazine* is an address for the opening of a new theater. His plea for applause for original plays written in democratic America is interesting in view of his own career as dramatist. Bird writes:

> Great Shakespeare tells us that—"a play's the thing
> With which to catch the conscience of a king,"

but he goes on to remark that

> In our republic,—in Columbia's clime
> *Kings* are extinguish'd, by "the tide of time"—
> While each bold yeoman, in his pride of birth,
> Stalks o'er the bosom of his parent earth,
>
> .   .   .   .
>
> You *all* are monarchs in creation's right,
> All *chartered freemen*, in the world's despite.

Thus it is to the general public, not to any king, that he appeals for consideration, and it is not for literature of the past but of the present that he makes his plea.

> 'Tis not for ages *past,* your voice we claim,
> Past times and nations had their meed of fame:
> We crave no laurels from the wreaths of Rome,
> *Honors,* like *charity*—begin at home.—
> The mighty dead the living but disgrace,
> Unless the living vindicate *their* place![3]

From about the same period (that is, 1825 to 1828, since several of the poems had been written several years earlier than they were published) come the humorous manuscript poem "Jemima," written for Bird's comedy *Bachelor's Hall,* and the four early poems printed in 1945 with Mary Mayer Bird's biography of her husband. Of these, "Melancholy's Allegories" is a weak expression of Byronic melancholy over the fact that, though he is young, the poet's life is over and the grave awaits him; "Health Song" is a slightly witty objurgation to drink like the ancients to the dead, like the moderns to the living. "Lines Written at Midnight" is a well-planned and controlled lyric, calling up through imagination the sepulchred dead and reminiscent of Bryant; and "Lines to the Wissahickon" is an even more Bryantesque poem about how, when tired of earth and mankind, one can turn to the beauty of nature for comfort:

> I dream of thee [the Wissahickon], when, tired of earth and men
> Thought needs a soother; when the opening day
> Sparkles with glory, and the night again
> Comes, like an Ethiop princess in array,
> Or the dead midnight holds his solemn sway,
> I think of thee, and how in such an hour
> Thou hast been to mine eye, with all thy gay,
> And melancholy, and contrasted power,
> Of rock, stream, star, and solitary bower.[4]

II Lyrics, Ballads, Patriotic Songs

From the middle period of Bird's life come most of the lyric poems that were anthologized. Three of these poems are about trees. "The Beech Tree," published in 1834 in *The Atlantic Club-Book*, is a singsongy lyric about sitting with a girl under a beech tree on the banks of the Schuylkill. "The China Tree," the result of Bird's trip South in 1833, was published in *The Knickerbocker* in 1835 and in the same year anthologized in *The Young Lady's Book of Elegant Poetry*. Though in the spring the South with its China trees, oranges, pomegranates, and humming birds seems like Elysium, the poet prefers the timid green leaves and bluebirds of the Northern spring. His heart turns toward home and those he loves there. The allusion to oaken chaplets is particularly happy:

> China tree! though thy blossoms, in chaplets, may bond
> The brows of the brave, and the necks of the fond,
> Never think that fit garlands our oak cannot form,
> For heads as majestic and bosoms as warm.[5]

The poem was a politely sentimental missive to send to Caroline and Mary Mayer, with whom he was corresponding during his trip.

The third poem in the arborical trio is "To an Old Sycamore, on the Banks of the Ohio," probably the result of one of Bird's sojourns in Cincinnati. It was published in 1835 in *The Young Man's Book of Elegant Poetry,* an anthology that aimed at "correct taste in morals, as well as in poetry" and that deplored the difficulty of finding passages of poetry "entirely free from objection on the score of moral purity." If it could speak, Bird says, the majestic ruin of the ancient sycamore tree could tell tales of Daniel Boone, captive maidens, and torture and death at the hands of Indians. But now the flood of immigration has washed away wild animals, Indians and wilderness; the tree now sees the magic city of Cincinnati, the Queen of the Ohio, "a scene of heaven." The poem is interesting in that, as in Cooper, it is difficult to ascertain where Bird's real sympathies lie. Does he more regret the passing of the romantic wilderness, the Indian, and the pioneer, or take pride in the swift peopling and progress of the country?

Another poem of this period is the vigorous ballad "The Romance of Cid Ramon," which was reprinted in *The Young Lady's Book* from the novel *Calavar.* In the poem Bird tells with great spirit an Irvingesque tale of a Moorish girl who refuses to turn Christian to win her lover but who, when it means death, accepts the Cross and dies with him. Bird's forte in poetry, as in prose, is not lyrical or sentimental or philosophical, but dramatic. "An Evening Ode" (beginning "O melancholy moon"), reprinted in the same anthology from *The Knickerbocker,* is a pointless lyric about a Byronic lover who cannot turn his heart to stone as he would wish and dies alone in a far country with only the moon as companion. "To a Child," published in *The Young Man's Book,* is a too sweet and unrealistic picture of a child as something that raises our thoughts to heaven from this world of woe. "Serenade," published in *The Book of Rubies* in 1866, long after Bird's death, and republished as late as 1874, is merely a conventional love poem.

Throughout his life one of Bird's interests was music. He himself played the flute; he copied much music; and he composed the lyrics and music for a great number of songs. He even projected several operas, one of them to be called "The Imp of the Rhine." In the 1830's he was very busy writing a series of patriotic songs or hymns and planned to issue a quarto volume of *Hymns of America*, of his own composition. Though a number of the lyrics are extant in manuscript, only one of these patriotic songs was published (1834) as sheet music under the title "God Bless America." In 1841 this song was included in the volume *American Melodies* compiled by George P. Morris, which was reissued in 1854 as *The Gift Book of American Melodies*. The lyrics of the song are trite: the Pilgrims came; the desert flowered; liberty and freedom grace America. The only interesting aspects are the topical references. In praying that no star or stripe shall disappear from the banner and in predicting the subsidence of "kingly states" into glorious union, Bird is obviously glancing at the Nullification controversy with which he had had first-hand acquaintance in Charleston in 1833. In the song he also expresses an opinion on slavery: Though a moderate on the question, he hopes that in the future no son of America will be a slave.

III *Longer Poems*

Three longer poems, no one of which was published, remain for comment. Two of these are vigorous narratives. One, "The Colapeesa," tells in rhymed verse the story of an Indian from a small tribe in Louisiana who is betrayed by the French to his enemies the Chocktaws. His old father takes his place and dies nobly in his stead. The picture of the Indian, interestingly enough in view of *Nick of the Woods* and *A Belated Revenge*, is the conventional eighteenth-century image of the noble, self-sacrificing savage. Bird seems later to have recast this story into a prose narrative.

The other narrative poem is "The Vestal, A Roman Story." In it a co-conspirator with Catiline, condemned to death by his unrelenting magistrate father, is saved by the pardon of a Vestal Virgin and becomes her slave. The play of feeling between the sternly just and patriotic father who refuses to pity his own son, and the Vestal Virgin who, though sworn to chastity, feels for the young man's good looks and tragic plight, is nicely delineated.

The third long poem was to have been Bird's poetic masterpiece. "The Cave" or "Mammoth Cave" is probably identical with the poems called in early notes "The Vision" and "The Alleghenies." It evidently grew over a long period of time, principal periods of composition being the summer of 1829 and the months of 1833 during which Bird was also working on *Calavar*. The plan was for a poem of nine cantos of twenty-seven Spenserian stanzas each. It was to deal with three of Bird's main interests: Mammoth Cave itself, American antiquities, and the political question of Nullification with its attendant dangers of civil strife.

"The Cave" begins with a description of the Allegheny Indians. The Wanderer, the principal character, comes to the cave and enters it with guides. Hoping that within the cave he can escape earth's troubles, he bids farewell to the world. Then follows a description of the great cave and of the Indian relics within it. In his exploration, however, the Wanderer becomes lost. In a vision he is roused by a phantom who shows him the Allegheny Indians vanishing one by one, each burying his predecessor, until the Wanderer's guide buries the last. The last four cantos were to be even more strictly allegorical (somewhat in the style of Paul Allen's *Noah*). Canto VI, for instance, set in the Hall of the Flood, was to describe allegorically the arrival of the Pilgrims, the settlement of the country, the importation of the Negroes, and the success of the Revolution. Canto VII was to describe the Hall of Heroes such as Napoleon, and the Hall of Immortals such as Washington. The last canto, to be placed in the Hall of Pillars, was to show through the figure of hammers destroying columns the successive falls of great nations and the danger threatening the United States through the secessionist tendencies of the Nullifiers. The Wanderer tries to stop the hammer that in the hands of the angel destroyer is about to smite down the column representing America. The poem was planned to permit Bird to include both description of scenery and narrative of speluncar adventure (a topic close to his heart), but the main motif was to be ethical and political. Bird's plan was to permit him either dramatically or directly to express his own deepest feelings about life and his country.

Though Bird characteristically made many notes and plans for the poem, the work was never completed. The poem as we have it in manuscript breaks off with Canto IV. Thus the parts on the cave itself and the exploring of the cave and its antiquities are extant, but the allegorical parts were only just begun. Bird usually found description and action easier than philosophizing.

Though Bird suggested that the unfinished poem be burnt at his death, his son Frederick Mayer Bird unsuccessfully tried, probably in the Centennial year 1876, to publish it as a patriotic "Centennial Poem." Of it he wrote, "Had the whole plan been carried out, the result might have been the most important of my father's works, and his best title to remembrance."[6] Even though a number of the Spenserian stanzas are fairly strong, it would be difficult for a modern critic to agree with Frederick Bird's high estimate. For what would undoubtedly have been the best parts —the descriptions of the cave—are less effective than the same material cast into the prose of the sketches of Mammoth Cave in *Peter Pilgrim*; and the unwritten allegorical parts, wrapped in their Byronic melancholy and prophetic mysticism, would have fitted neither Bird's real talents nor modern taste.

CHAPTER 3

Early Plays

P RACTICALLY every major British author of the early nineteenth century tried his hand at writing plays. Scott, Words-
worth, Coleridge, Lamb, Byron, Shelley, Keats, Tennyson, and
Browning—all attempted poetic drama. In America the so-called
Elizabethan or Romantic Revival of drama was not so widespread, partly because of the general moral prejudice against the
theater, especially in the eastern parts of the United States. But
Longfellow wrote his *Spanish Student* and his *Christus;* Poe his
fragmentary *Politian;* and a host of forgotten authors made other
attempts at dramatic writing. Few of these primarily literary
authors, whether British or American, wrote works that were
successful on the stage. Most of them were trying the impossible.
They were attempting to write Elizabethan drama in the
nineteenth century; they were using a Shakespearean language
that had not been spoken for over two hundred years; and they
were led astray by anthologies of selections from the old
dramatists into thinking that every passage should be a purple
passage. Most important, in the majority of cases they were
trying to write plays without knowing anything about the real
conditions and requirements of the theater.

When during his last year of medical school and his year of
medical practice Robert Montgomery Bird began to write plays,
he carried on this tradition of Elizabethan Revival closet drama.
It is true that the theater was a living force in the Philadelphia
of his time—soon the city was to be the center of a group of native
playwrights—and that in some instances he undoubtedly aimed
at actual theatrical production of his plays. Some of the manuscripts, indeed, show marks of having been sent to managers
for consideration (though whether before or after his success
with *The Gladiator* is difficult to say). Yet Bird's earliest plays
belong in general to the literary tradition. Bird has studied

carefully his Shakespeare, his Elizabethan and Jacobean, and even some of the Restoration dramatists. He evidently knew Ben Jonson well. In his own plays he imitates the works of these playwrights. He uses the impossibly archaic, pseudo-Elizabethan language thought proper for drama in the 1820's and 1830's, and his poetic dramas are in semi-Shakespearean blank verse. The settings of the plays, as was the general custom in most of the closet drama and much of the acting drama of the period, are in romantic foreign lands—Italy, Germany, and Spain. Both comic and tragic characters are highly conventional; one could easily find their counterparts in the old plays. The plots are complicated and depend in large part on impossible disguise and mistaken identity. If one is to read these dramas and fragments with pleasure, one must try to put oneself back into an age when imitation of the Shakespearean or Restoration tradition was applauded rather than derided. And one must remember that they are the apprentice work of a young man of only twenty-one or twenty-two.

I Early Comedies

Whether Bird tried his hand first at comedy or at tragedy it is impossible to tell. Only one of the early comedies–*The City Looking Glass* (July, 1828)—can be dated. (The date 1827 that appears on the first page of the manuscript of *'Twas All for the Best* is actually not the date of the play but that of a draft letter across which the play was written; elsewhere on the manuscript is the penciled notation "generally 1833.") Nor does there seem to be very much progression in skill among them. Probably, however, the two very slight fragmentary comedies *Bachelor's Hall, or All in a Hobble* and *The Masque of the Devils, or The Canterbury Clock* antedate the others. Neither is of any value.

'Twas All for the Best is a conventional comedy of manners imitative, as Arthur Hobson Quinn remarks, of Congreve at his feeblest.[1] Much of it was completed, though the latter parts are only sketched in. Though it is set in England, the characters speak a language never heard on land or sea except in the nineteenth-century theater. As in Restoration comedy, the characters' names (for instance, that of Sluggardly, the innkeeper) indicate their personalities. There is much supposed

humor, including a number of awkward puns. The plot, which is far too complicated to be clear, centers on the character of Sir Noel Nozlebody, who in his well-intentioned absurdity goes so far as to steal his brother's daughter, bring her up as his own child, and call his own daughter a foundling. Everything that he does is wrong, but all is done for the best reasons. The character of Sir Noel is so entirely beyond all belief and his actions so utterly improbable that the play has no real effect. Bird has not yet learned that absurdity in drama must be the exaggeration of the real rather than the creation of the impossible, and in the heart-rending separation of father and daughter his comedy is too close to tragedy to be truly amusing. As in most of Bird's dramas, the lower-class characters are weakly conventional. At one time, whether at the time of composition or later, Bird evidently submitted the manuscript to William Wood, manager of the Chestnut Street Theater in Philadelphia, with suggestions as to which actors should take the various parts.

From the same general period comes *News of the Night,* a completely farcical comedy, which has the complicated plot usually favored by Bird. It concerns two sets of lovers, a guardian uncle who wishes his nieces to elope so that he may pocket half of their inheritance, and a great box into which at various times a number of the characters find their way, to be toted by porters in and out of various houses, usually the wrong houses at the wrong time. Originally the poor debtor Ha'penny, pursued by bailiffs, was evidently to have been the central figure, for an early synopsis is entitled *The Man without Money;* but in the completed play his is only a minor part. Agony, the miserly uncle, is in the end not only done out of the inheritance he longs for but is forced into marriage with his housekeeper. The two pairs of lovers are at last rightly paired and married.

Though the scene is Philadelphia, the plot is out of Plautus or Terence by way of Ben Jonson, and characters are in large part "humour" characters in the Jonsonian sense. The play moves quickly; the "mistakes of the night" are funny; the farcical situations are playable; there is considerable skill in plotting. But on the whole the play has no real point, is artificial, and the properties—girls dressed as men, old chests, rope ladders, and the like—are conventional. Interesting in the light of Bird's later use of dialect in his novels is the almost "Western" humor of the boasting of Margaret when she is pretending to be her midshipman brother: Ralph Stackpole of *Nick of the Woods* is faintly foreshadowed. A lacuna in the play was filled when in 1958 Richard Harris found a missing scene from Act I mistakenly bound with another manuscript play and restored it to its rightful place.[2] *News of the Night* was played for the first time by the Columbia Laboratory Players at the McMillin Theater in New York on November 2, 1929.[3]

Though *The City Looking Glass* (manuscript dated July, 1829) has been hailed by Quinn as an important early example in America of the dramatic treatment of low life in a large city,[4] it too is highly derivative; and, aside from some sectional humor, it is little more American than Ben Jonson's *Bartholomew Fair*. The plot involves some rogues, Ravin and Ringfinger, who plot to gain possession of two girls, one of whom—Emma—is thought to be the daughter of a bawd but who (of course) is found by the discovery of a portrait, a necklace, and a birthmark to be really the respectable daughter stolen in early childhood from a wealthy Virginian planter. The evidence for her chastity, however, is not so good as for her birth. Some of the action is cleverly planned for stage effect, but the conventions of the foundling girl, the villains who explain their villainy to the audience, the stage language, and the pseudo-Elizabethan fool make the play seem too long. The only real life comes to the play with the entrance in Act IV of Raleigh, the fire-eating Virginia squire, who has amusingly exaggerated Southern views on slavery, the tariffs, and states' rights. But the contemporary references, on the whole, are few, though the picture of Raleigh's father arriving in Philadelphia with a platoon of Negro slaves in livery gives an interesting insight into the times. *The City Looking Glass* was produced for the first time on January 20, 1933, by the Zelosophic Society of the University of Pennsylvania.

II *Early Tragedies*

Of the numerous tragedies which Bird planned to write in these early years there remain fragments of five and plans for others like *King Philip, or the Sagamore* and *Men of the Hills* (which was later turned into a story and thence into a novel: several of Bird's stories and novels were first planned as plays). The three shorter fragments are all in archaic language; blank verse is used for more noble characters; prose for the lower. *The Fanatick*, based in part on Charles Brockden Brown's novel *Wieland*, is set in Germany in a time after the Reformation when many strange sects were arising. A baron who is a religious fanatic is played upon by the villain and persuaded by fake miracles that he should found a new religion. The villain, by murdering his own wife and the baron's son, hopes to obtain for himself the baron's wife, after whom he lusts, and the baron's property. This was the plan for the play, but actually only a few inchoate fragments were written.

Another of these fragments, *The Three Dukes, or the Lady of Catalonia*, sometimes referred to as *Isidora* or *The Duke and the Gypsy*, has a Spanish setting. One lover, Palador, grieves because his beloved, Angela, is too loving; the other, Duke Rafael, grieves because his, Isidora, seems too cold, though she actually dotes on him. From this basis the plot, which Bird changed several times, was to have been built up to a tragic climax of poison and death. One wordy, slow act was completed; two others exist in summaries. The scene of the third fragment, *Giannone*, is near Naples. The younger brother of the usurping Duke villainously plots to kill both his own supposedly peasant-born wife and the Duke, for the plotter wishes to marry the princess affianced to his brother and to inherit the kingdom. But he is foiled by the return of the real Duke, who had been banished by the petulant king, and by the reformation of his villainous tool Riccardi. The two completed acts of this bloody drama have a good deal of spirit. In fact, it is the best of the fragments.

Like these fragments, the two completed or nearly completed tragedies are in the melodramatic mode of the time. Like them, they are imitated from the Elizabethans and Jacobeans. *The Cowled Lover*, dated in manuscript June, 1827, has the poetic "high" scenes, the "humorous" low scenes in prose, the lyrics to be sung, and all the conventions of disguise characteristic of that tradition. In plot it is modeled on *Romeo and Juliet*. Raymond, in love with Rosalia, daughter of a bitter enemy of his house, disguises himself as a monk (hence the title) to enter the, to him, deadly castle where she is feigning madness to avoid being wed to Vincentio, whom her father favors. As a result of the shrewd penetration of Raymond's disguise by a servant of Vincentio, both Raymond and Rosalia are killed by Rosalia's father. Though Bird successfully builds up a great deal of suspense, the fault of the play is that the tragedy is not dependent on character (as it is, to some extent at least, in Shakespeare's play) but purely on circumstance. Indeed, there is no real characterization. Another major flaw in the plot is that for no apparent reason the hero runs off, leaving his loyal foster brother Florio to be slaughtered for lack of his assistance. He also leaves Rosalia to be stabbed by her father. It is interesting to note even so early as this the weakness of the ostensible hero which undermines the effect of *The Hawks of Hawk Hollow* and others of Bird's later prose romances.

In addition to the strong Elizabethan strain, the play, like Shelley's *Cenci* or Byron's *Manfred*, has many Gothic elements, such as monkish disguise and murder of child by father. The hero himself is very much in the Byronic tradition. He is, he says, "earth's outcast, orphaned by the fates." He will hold to his love though he must defy the wrathful heavens. He is alone in the world, and he brings death on all those whom he loves. Again, like a good Romantic, Bird puts into his hero's mouth several declamatory speeches on liberty and freedom. But such rhetoric he will include much more effectively in his major tragedies.

Caridorf, though it has more of an underlying idea than most of these early plays in that it is aimed against duelling, also fails because the melodramatic action does not arise out of real psychological portrayal. The central character and the ostensible hero is Caridorf. We are asked to believe that, aside from a "demon" in his breast, he is essentially good and admirable. But it is difficult to admire or feel sympathy with a man who refuses to come to solace a dying father; who, having seduced Genevra, will not marry her nor trust her, since by his own act, she is not chaste; who, when Ludovick challenges him to a duel, arranges to have him captured by robbers; who will not trust his brother and has him killed; and who finally poisons Genevra herself. He is thoroughly despicable, an utter villain; and yet Bird wants us to feel for him even though no understandable explanation is given for his demonic villainy. Caridorf treads a downward path, yet it does not seem even to be fate that drives him on. All seems unmotivated.

The other major characters have even less reality. Genevra is the conventional nineteenth-century fallen woman who, though she is essentially good and innocent, can never rise or be trusted or respected again. The fall from virtue, according to Bird, tears away the keystone of the arch of a woman's morality and undermines all other parts of the structure. To the twentieth century, the verbiage about death being the only refuge of the unchaste seems both tiresome and foolish. Lillio is a foolish Jonsonian "humour" character, and nothing is made of Ludovick, Genevra's brother. The minor characters are wholly conventional. The only one who has a spark of life is the murdering bravo, the hired assassin, who with satiric wit claims that murder is his trade, a trade like any other, and that therefore he, as an instrument of others' crime, is not more guilty than his sword. The rest of the wit and punning in the play falls flat.

By the end of 1829, the date we can consider that most of these plays and fragments had been carried to the degree of completion in which we now have them, Robert Montgomery Bird had shown few signs of any real talent for drama. A few passages in blank verse fall well on the ear; there is some ability to conceive situations that would be comic on the stage; *The Cowled Lover* builds up considerable suspense; several of the fragments show fecundity in plotting. Yet most of the early dramatic work is highly imitative and highly conventional—just what many a young man of Bird's era with a taste for literature and the theater would have been likely to write. Bird, however, had shown unusual pertinacity in sticking to his dramatic attempts; within one or two years he had written much and had planned an enormous amount more. It was evident that he was seriously interested in a literary career. But, in order to write effectively for the theater, he needed a chance for real production of his plays. He needed the encouragement and advice of someone with actual personal knowledge of the theater. He needed an actor for whom to write. All these he was to find through Edwin Forrest. But Bird needed, in addition, one more ingredient: he needed a cause or an idea. This he was to find in liberty.

CHAPTER 4

Classical Plays

IN THE HISTORY of early nineteenth-century American stage tragedy the figure of Edwin Forrest (1806-72) looms large. Not only was he one of the most popular and able tragic actors of the day but he was also a powerful force in encouraging American playwrighting. It was he who stimulated Robert Montgomery Bird to his major dramatic work, who brought Bird fame by acting his plays with great success both in America and in England, and who, unfortunately, finally turned Bird away from playwrighting in disillusionment and disgust.

In 1828, following the custom of a number of well-known actors of the time, Edwin Forrest began to offer annual prizes to American playwrights for plays suitable for production by him. For the next seven years he continued the practice and revived it again in the year 1847. More than two hundred plays were submitted, of which nine received prizes. Twenty thousand dollars is said to have been paid contestants. At first the hero or principal character had to be a native American, but in later years that stipulation was removed. Of the nine plays given prizes, four were by Bird (though in actual fact he received only three prizes, *The Gladiator* being substituted for *Pelopidas*). The others were John Augustus Stone's *Metamora* and *The Ancient Briton*, Richard Penn Smith's *Caius Marius*, Robert T. Conrad's *Jack Cade*, and George H. Miles's *Mohammed*.[1] All these playwrights were residents of Philadelphia: by his contests the great Philadelphia actor encouraged a group of Philadelphia authors who made that city the center of America playwrighting in the early 1830's. In one sense the contests were a devious scheme which enabled Forrest to obtain for a pittance dramas written especially for him and from which he could make hundreds of thousands of dollars; nevertheless, he did encourage through them the writing of some of the best American tragedies of the time. Among these were Bird's.

Forrest's achievement in stimulating the writing of so many American tragedies is striking in that, aside from Thomas Godfrey's *Prince of Parthia*, William Dunlap's plays, and perhaps James Barker's *Indian Princess* and *Superstition,* little American tragedy of any value had hitherto been written. Indeed, if we may believe Bird himself, the theater was at a low ebb. In 1831, just before the resounding success of his *Gladiator,* he wrote in his *Secret Records* that theatrical audiences were foolish and vulgar. Anyone who wrote for the theater must write for the mob, for cultured people did not go to the theater. Moreover, the actors themselves were often ignorant and incompetent. In another manuscript fragment entitled "The Decline of Drama" Bird listed three main reasons why good drama was not being written. First, authors refused to submit to the ignorance and brutality of the audiences and to the malice and meanness of the critics; second, in the theater genius was placed at the mercy of the mob; and, third, other literary employments offered more rewards.[2] Much of what Bird said was true, though its truth certainly was not confined to the American theater: the same complaints of drunken actors, shabby properties, and riotous audiences could equally well have been made in England. But under the aegis of a few leading actors and courageous writers, Romantic drama was beginning to come into its own. In Germany, Schiller had written his *Wallenstein* and *Maria Stuart* and Goethe the first part of *Faust;* in France, Hugo was writing *Cromwell, Hernani,* and *Le roi s'amuse;* and, best parallel of all, in England Forrest's great rival William Charles Macready was working closely with Bulwer on *The Lady of Lyons, Richelieu,* and *Money* and would soon encourage the youthful Robert Browning toward dramatic writing. The revival of tragedy in Philadelphia, though certainly owing much to Forrest, was part of a widespread literary movement.

I *Dramatic Traditions in America*

Even in the brief course of this Romantic revival of playwrighting in America certain traditions and trends developed which are important to an understanding of Bird's works. One of these was a fondness for the picturing of a patriotic hero struggling proudly against despotism, with implied overtones of the liberty-loving American revolting against Old World tyranny. Most of Forrest's prize plays were of this semipatriotic nature, though the trend had begun before his contests. Tragic heroes of the time were Brutus, the man who defied the Tarquins (John Howard Payne, *Brutus; or, The Fall of Tarquin,* 1818); Sertorius, the Roman patriot who fought the tyranny of Sulla (David P. Brown, *Sertorius; or, the Roman Patriot,* 1830); King Philip, the brave Indian warrior who resisted the encroachments of the Puritans (John A. Stone, *Metamora,* 1829); and even Jack Cade, the fifteenth-century English rebel (Robert T. Conrad, *Jack Cade, the Captain of the Commons,* 1835). Earlier, William Dunlap had written about William Tell, the Swiss patriot.[3] Bird's Athenian patriot Pelopidas revolting against Spartan tyranny, his noble slave Spartacus leading a rebellion against the cruel Romans, and his high-souled Inca Oralloossa bravely opposing the conquering Spaniards in Peru all belong in this tradition.

A second tradition was that of the Indian play, and of that more will be said when *Oralloossa* is considered. A third tradition was that of the Classical play—that is, the play which centered upon a hero such as Brutus or Sertorius. Richard Penn Smith wrote a tragedy on *Caius Marius;* Jonas B. Phillips wrote *Camillus;* and the Classical plays of the English dramatist Sheridan Knowles were very popular in America. Bird was therefore following a well-defined custom when he took the Greek Pelopidas and the Roman Spartacus as his heroes and read their stories as righteous struggles against the oppression of foreign conquerors and aristocratic masters. In the strong nineteenth-century tradition common not only to drama but to poetry and the historical novel as well, he used history for political and social comment about his own day. Bird's practice was to join this general and political feeling with a powerful domestic theme. In *Pelopidas* it is the hero's love for his wife and son that causes him almost to fail his country. In *The Gladiator,* similarly, Spartacus becomes a gladiator only to ransom his wife and child. This kind of theme, of course, rises to its climax in Bird's works in *The Broker of Bogota;* in it he gave up history in order to concentrate solely on the old broker's relationship with his son.

II *Bird's Theories of Drama*

Bird's own theories of dramatic composition were also important in shaping his major plays. He took the profession of playwright seriously. The good dramatist, he wrote in his *Secret Records,* needed invention, imagination and poetic fancy, common sense, fiery ardor, phlegmatic judgment, an ability to feel the extremes of passion, cold-blooded philosophy, and intuitive knowledge of human nature. He had to be able not only to create but to imagine his creation being acted on the stage. For, whereas it was easy to write blank-verse closet drama (such as he had himself written earlier), he had found that it was hard to write a good stage play. A good stage play could be written only by a man who had both the gift of poetry and a knack for dramatic effect. The stage dramatist, he therefore believed, was of a higher order than the mere closet dramatist, who was often wrongly praised at the former's expense.

In a long passage quoted by Foust in his life of Bird, Bird expanded on the criteria for good drama:

> The true secret of effect [in drama] consists in having everything as well in details as in general structure epigrammatic or climacteric, the story rising to rapidity and closing with power; the chief characters increasing in passion and energy; the events growing in interest, the scenes and acts each accumulating power above their percursors; the strength of a speech augmenting at its close, and the important characters dismissed at each exit with some sort of point and emphasis. The first part of the education of a dramatist is that which fits him to be a writer; the second makes him an actor; the third inducts him into the principles of criticism; and he has completed his studies when he can exercise the functions of the three not separately but together.

Then Bird turned to the function and training of the actor, but what he said on that subject reflected also on the task of the dramatist. Again he emphasized knowledge of the theater. Like that of the playwright, "the education of an actor can only be acquired in the theater, and in a close study of great plays. First he must learn 'stage business,' comprising the mechanical aspects of the actor's art, the management of voice, gestures, grouping, and so on. He must then learn to act with effect and to see in our great dramas 'what it is that is effective.' " Then turning again to the playwright, Bird continued:

> He will perceive that certain incidents and situations and certain forms of language are impressive on the boards; while others, perhaps not less interesting and beautiful in imagination, are entirely without point in performance. The great, perhaps the chief, secret of effect depends upon the style of language. . . . The secret is simple: that writer stumbles upon dramatic effect whose characters speak like men; and he fails whose personages declaim like orators and poets. We sympathize in a theater with nothing that is not natural; we even feel the homeliest expressions of passion, when they are like those of the beings around us. . . . Shakespeare is a greater dramatist than others because he is more natural. Nature is unchangeable; and at this day . . . Othello speaks in language more akin to that of our fellows than his classic shadow, Zampa. The human expression that breathes from the lips of Lear and Macbeth would render them heirlooms on the stage, [even] had they been otherwise on a level with the other writings of the day.[4]

Whether Bird had the qualities he considered necessary to the dramatist and whether his plays, despite their frequently oratorical character, have the touch of nature that leads to immortality must be decided by each reader of Bird's tragedies. But one fact is plain: Bird did learn to adopt his plays to the theater. Since his mentor was Edwin Forrest, the qualities that Bird's plays have are those that Forrest particularly liked and required. The dramas were not only written for Forrest; Forrest himself took an active part in their shaping and revision. The manuscripts of several of the plays show the penciled comments he made as he read them scene by scene and suggested how they could be better adapted to his capabilities and the requirements of scenic presentation. His preferences, his personality, his prejudices, and his style of acting in large part determined what kind of plays Bird (and also the other Philadelphia dramatists) wrote.

Forrest's style was not a subtle one. He loved the panoramic scene, the picturesque attitude, the high-flown sentiment about freedom or country. He liked the grand pose and the great speech, the grand address. His acting was oratorical—sometimes it degenerated into rant. He particularly liked to play a role of a fiery nature, in which he could give expression to vigorous sarcasm, lofty pride, deep hatred, passionate love, and inspired ecstacy. As Montrose Moses expresses it in his biography of Forrest, the actor wanted his dramas to provide a series of exercises in intense emotions—tender, defiant, pathetic, triumphant.[5] He aimed more at mass applause than at critical acclaim.

He was obsessed with physical fitness (Mary Bird suggests that a common interest in sports and athletics was one of the bonds between Forrest and her husband during the years of their close friendship), and he loved to show off his splendid torso and his muscular calves and thighs. Thus roles such as those of a Roman gladiator stripped for the arena or an Indian warrior appareled for battle appealed to him greatly. As a star, and a jealous one, Forrest naturally also insisted that the part which he played should be a large and controlling one. Hence his objection to *Pelopidas,* in which the hero is but one of several noble conspirators and in which the part of Philidas really outshines his. In *The Gladiator* and *Oralloossa,* and to a lesser extent in *The Broker of Bogota,* Bird skillfully and successfully gave him the big part, the orotund speeches, the noble sentiments, and searing emotions that he demanded. One wonders what kind of plays Bird could have written for an actor of another type.

Before beginning to write Bird always read widely on the subject he had chosen. Indeed, he did a great deal of research for his historical plays. Though *Pelopidas* is based almost wholly on the account of the Athenian hero in Plutarch's *Lives* (Bird makes several changes in the story to heighten the dramatic effectiveness of his play), the list of authorities consulted for *The Gladiator* is long and learned. In addition to Plutarch, Bird read Livy, Florus, Eutropius, Velleius Paterculus, and Appian, as well as the modern historians Ferguson and Hooke (from whom he probably obtained many of the Classical references). He also looked up articles on Spartacus in *Blackwood's Magazine. Oralloossa* and *The Broker* are based on his very wide reading and long study of the history of Spanish America. Having read widely and taken notes—there are many scrapbooks full of such notes among Bird's papers—Bird ordinarily made a prose résumé of the plot of his play. This he divided into acts and scenes. Thereupon he began his writing. He used the same method in writing his novels and even his long poem "The Cave". This similarity of approach made it easy for him to change a subject which he had originally planned as a play or poem into material for a story or a novel.

III *Pelopidas*

The first of Bird's major plays was *Pelopidas; or, The Fall of the Polemarchs*. Finished in 1830, it was accepted by Forrest as a prize play but was never produced. In 1840 William E. Burton, manager of the National Theater in Philadelphia, offered to produce it on terms very advantageous to Bird—eight hundred dollars for the first night or ten per cent of gross receipts nightly. Burton's plan was to bring it out on the same night on which Forrest was opening in Robert T. Conrad's *Jack Cade*. But Bird declined, saying that he wanted no rivalry with Forrest and had no wish to compete with Conrad. Bird's son printed a title page in 1868; but because of Forrest's claim to copyright the play was not published until Foust's edition in 1919.

Pelopidas shows an immense advance over the earlier plays. It deals with the period in Thebes when the Spartans had taken control of the city and had installed four dictatorial polemarchs as governors. Exiled Pelopidas, the great Theban patriot, secretly returns to the city to overthrow the Spartan government and to restore the city to its citizens. He is stimulated to his plot by the news that one of the polemarchs has been attempting to seduce his wife Sibylla, who is still in the city. The conspiracy almost goes awry when Pelopidas hurries to attempt the rescue of his wife and is captured. But he manages to escape in time to take part in the destruction of the polemarchs at a banquet to which they have been lured by Philidas, one of their number, who is really in sympathy with the rebels. Suspense is built up as Philidas again and again barely prevents the Spartans from being warned of their danger and as the conspirators delay the attack. Pelopidas, however, finally arrives, dispatches the tyrants, and then races off to the citadel just in time to save his son and Sibylla from being murdered by Leontidas.

Bird strengthens the story as told by Plutarch by making two of the polemarchs Spartan. This change allows an interesting differentiation between the attitude of the foreign or Spartan tyrants Archias and Philip and the native tyrants Leontidas and Philidas. Bird further differentiates within these pairs: of the foreign tyrants Archias is the indolent, carefree Spartan, never suspecting evil; Philip is the active, suspicious Spartan. Of the native tyrants Leontidas is the thorough renegade who is attempting to seduce or force Pelopidas' wife; Philidas, who really turns out to be the most effective character in the drama, plays the part of turncoat but is in truth patriotically assisting the rebels.

Bird does a fairly good job, too, of giving his characters individuality. Though Pelopidas is brave, his rashness in going to see his wife nearly brings disaster to his whole plot. Leontidas is cynical and hard. Philidas is cool and self-controlled despite his danger in being one of the conspirators in the midst of the Spartans. The part of Sibylla—the wife left amid her husband's enemies, courted by her formerly rejected lover Leontidas, worried over the safety of her son, yet true in heart and action to her absent husband—has emotional appeal. There is some attempt to characterize the minor characters such as Laon, the doubter and coward who reveals the plot to the Spartans.

Much of the effect of the play, however, rests on suspense and high sentiment. Again and again, largely through the foolishness of Pelopidas (Bird's heroes are almost all rash and foolish and we wonder whether they should have been chosen as heroes), the plot is almost discovered. Pelopidas himself is detected and imprisoned; all is nearly lost. The suspense comes to a climax in the highly effective banquet scene, in which Philidas calmly baffles the repeated efforts of the Spartans to warn the polemarch Archias of his danger until it is too late and the Thebans can take control. This is the striking scene of the play. The final rescue by Pelopidas of his son and Sibylla from the grasp of the murderous and lustful Leontidas, though a resounding conclusion, is more melodrama than drama. We wonder, indeed, whether the play would not have been more effective if it had been written as a true tragedy, ending in the triumph of the Thebans, but only after the death of Pelopidas and his family. However, writing in an age when *King Lear* was played with a happy ending, Bird probably did not wish his play to terminate so grimly. Throughout the play the revolt of the Thebans against their oppressors permits a great deal of lofty democratic rhetoric; and the conclusion of the play, with its anti-slavery sentiment, looks forward to the feeling of *The Gladiator*. But Forrest's criticisms on the manuscript are just.

The first three acts, he said, lack incident; more bustling and action are needed. Some of the speeches are too long. Act III, he thought, needs a stronger climax; and, while Act IV and Act V are generally good as they are, the play should conclude more quickly.[6]

IV *The Gladiator*

Bird's next play was the resounding success of his life and one of the most popular plays ever written and produced in America. On its first performance in New York City on September 26, 1831, *The Gladiator* scored an instant triumph. Though Bird thought the performance "a horrid piece of bungling from beginning to end," even he had only praise for Forrest's acting. With better scenery, costumes, and supporting actors, the play overwhelmed Philadelphia where it was produced on October 24. In November the play scored a resounding success in Boston. Everywhere, despite a few adverse comments, the general tone of the reviews was favorable. It was called "the best native tragedy extant." It was said to bear "the stamp of genius in every lineament." It was thought to be better than Payne's *Brutus* or Knowles's *Virginius.* Its beautiful passages, noble sentiments, and intense passion were lauded, as well as its "strictness to historical truth in all its details."[7] Wemyss, the Philadelphia critic, thought it "the perfection of melodramatic tragedy."[8]

But *The Gladiator* was no flash in the pan tremendously successful at first, then immediately forgotten. It held the stage for over seventy years. By 1854 it had had over one thousand performances; it was said to be the first play in the English language to be performed so often within the lifetime of the author. After Bird's death it retained its popularity. Forrest kept it in his active repertoire till he retired from the stage. Macready, the great English tragic actor, performed in it. After Forrest's death John McCullough played in it frequently. As late as 1893 Robert Downing was acting in it at the Grand Opera House in New York.[9] It was one of the greatest hits America has ever seen.

Much of the immediate popularity of the play was due to Edwin Forrest's acting. The play precisely fitted him. It gave him an opportunity to display his muscles, and on his first appearance on the stage the audience burst into applause at the sight of him in his scanty costume. The play also had all the melodramatic passion that Forrest loved and was able to portray so well. It gave full rein to all the elemental emotions—pathos, fierce passion, doting love, and rending grief. It let Forrest stand, as he loved to stand (in Montrose Moses' words), as "the insurgent figure alone, subject to humiliation, giving way before necessity," withstanding suffering because of high-minded affection, rebelling at last, and dying in statuesque lines.[10] Forrest's Spartacus, the actor James Rees says, was considered "the perfection of the art histrionic."[11] Rarely, indeed, has a playwright been so successful in supplying an actor with a part. The importance of Forrest's contribution to the success of the play is evidenced by the fact that when Forrest opened in it in London on his first tour to England in 1836, the critics praised the actor but disliked the play; and, when Forrest tried to speak words of praise for Bird, the audience drowned him out with cries of "Give us Shakespeare." Yet Bird had given Forrest the opportunity to show his power as an actor by providing him (as Forrest wished) with a play concentrated almost wholly on a single role—a concentration that Forrest intensified by his judicious revision of Bird's play for the stage representation.

The play opens with Phasarius and other gladiators pondering revolt against a Rome now weakened by the absence of its generals and troops. However, Phasarius postpones his plans for revolt until he can meet and conquer a new gladiator, a Thracian recently captured, who is said to be a better fighter even than Phasarius himself. This new warrior is Spartacus, who consents to fight only in order to free his wife and child from slavery. When the two men face each other, they recognize each other as brothers, fall on each other's necks, and rouse the other gladiators to revolt. In the ensuing war the gladiator army is highly successful until Phasarius and Spartacus begin to disagree; Phasarius desires to ravage Rome, Spartacus merely to return to his homeland. Their disagreement is heightened to mutiny when Spartacus protects from Phasarius' advances Julia, daughter of the Roman consul, whom the slaves have captured. The Romans defeat and massacre the divided servile armies. Through the treachery of Phasarius, Spartacus' wife and child are slain. Spartacus refuses a pardon from the Romans and, encircled and desperate but heroic in his rage, dies sword in hand.

For the story of the Thracian gladiator who gathered a great army of slaves, defeated a consul, and almost conquered the great city of Rome, Bird turned, as has been said, to various authorities. But he used history only as inspiration; he changed the historical facts in order to make a living, meaningful human story. Indeed, the whole spirit of the drama is highly unhistorical. The real Spartacus certainly never had such obviously nineteenth-century ideals of humanity, democracy, and freedom as does Bird's character. And for a Thracian shepherd of the first century B.C., Spartacus has somewhere picked up an amazing knowledge of history and geography. The real sources of the drama, then, are not the historical but the literary ones. The general theme probably was inspired by the play *Caius Marius* by Bird's fellow-Philadelphian, Richard Penn Smith. The amphitheatre scene was already hoary in poems and plays and novels about Rome and especially about Pompeii.[12] And the play is in the then international tradition of dramas about classical subjects used by writers patriotically to laud freedom and to attack tyranny.

Much of the difference between this play and the shadowy closet dramas of Bird's first period of playwriting lies in the fact that it has a cause, an idea and ideal. Spartacus, as Quinn points out, is representative of the eternal struggle of the common man for freedom from tyranny, and this theme gives the play its meaning. But the play has even more specific applicability to the American situation. It is anti-imperialistic and therefore, like many of the American plays of the period, anti-British by implication. The great and wealthy Roman empire is cruel, corrupt, and built on the misery of the vanquished. It ravages its faraway colonies. Revolt against it (shades of the American Revolution) is therefore laudable. *The Gladiator* is also anti-aristocratic. Writing only a few years after the inauguration of Andrew Jackson, Bird strongly supports the noble but perhaps rough slave-hero from the wilds of Thrace against the rich and well-born Romans. He thinks that the virtue and new blood of the poor is better than ancient lineage. In an obvious reflection of current American politics, he raises the question whether it is right that only the wealthy are permitted to govern.

The major contemporary note that Bird was striking, however, was that of slavery. In the year when William Lloyd Garrison was establishing *The Liberator*, Bird was filling the first act of his play with Abolitionism—"as full of 'Abolitionism,'" Walt

Whitman wrote, "as an egg is of meat."[13] He struck at the selling of slaves, flogging, the parting of families, and the assumption that one race (whether Thracian or Negro) is inferior to another. Perhaps his bitterest comment is on the condoning by religion, whether pagan or Christian, of the institution of slavery. Bird was himself conscious of the relevance of his play to the contemporary situation. "If the *Gladiator* were produced in a slave state," he wrote, "the managers, players, and perhaps myself in the bargain, would be rewarded with the Penitentiary!"

Yet it is interesting that, though his Thracian rebels are pictured as noble and generous, Bird had no such ideas about the Negro slaves of America. In the same passage in which he points out the relevance of *The Gladiator*, he goes on to comment that, as he writes, six to eight hundred rebelling slaves under Nat Turner are murdering, ravishing, and burning in Virginia. "If they had had a Spartacus among them," Bird remarks, "to organize the half million of Virginia, the hundreds of thousands of the [other] states, and lead them on in the Crusade of Massacre, what a blessed example might they not give to the world of the excellence of slavery!" He predicts a slave rebellion in the United States which will make Haiti's look like a farce, for violence breeds violence. Again his bitterest comment is against the church: if at the start of Turner's rebellion most of the white men had not been away from home at a prayer-meeting, the revolt with its ravage would probably not have started at all.[14] Revolt by Thracian gladiators in Rome and by American Negroes in Virginia are, we gather, two different matters; what is a situation for poetic eloquence in drama may be a scene of horror and brutality in real life. Bird can see the Thracian warrior as the noble work of God, formed far from the vices of the city by the beneficent forces of rural nature; he can imagine him equal or superior to the noblest and best of the cultured Romans. (Again in Bird's next play, *Oralloossa*, the Inca is noble and good, and most of the Spaniards corrupt and treacherous.) But for Bird the Negro slave of Virginia, though joyous and happy and good when a loyal servant to a good master, is a murderous savage when he strikes for his freedom.

As a stage play in the melodramatic tradition *The Gladiator* was deservedly a mighty success. The end of Act II, when the gladiators recognize each other as brothers, refuse to fight each other, and call on all the other gladiators and slaves to strike for freedom, was evidently almost without parallel in sensational effect. The quarrel of Spartacus and Phasarius, the return of Phasarius humbled and contrite, and the death of Spartacus as he fights alone at the end against the conquering Romans, also make powerful scenes. As a vehicle for Forrest and as a drama providing opportunity for striking tableaux and powerful scenic effects the play is superbly devised. Though it is in an heroic and melodramatic tradition foreign to twentieth-century taste, we can understand its long success on the stage. But, as Bird himself said of *The Gladiator*, in it "as in most tragedies, the silliest and most ridiculous portions are the best for the theater, because they always draw the greatest applause."[15] Bird also at one time dismissed his play as "full of blood and thunder."[16]

The question, then, is whether it has literary as well as scenic value. When *The Gladiator* was first presented, the main criticism of it was that the climax came too early. The highest point in the play, at least as it is acted, is at the end of Act II. Much of the rest of the play, especially Act III, seemed to many critics anticlimactic and pedestrian. This fault does not loom so large in the play when it is read. For, as Quinn says, Bird moves from the climax of action in the amphitheater scene to a climax of character when Spartacus must make his decision between success and honor and when he must bear the news of his wife's death and his own doom.[17] It is true, however, as the theatrical critics also said, that the play is in large part a one-character play. The whole interest of it depends on Spartacus; the other characters are conventional or shadowy. Whether Spartacus himself is real and believable is a matter of opinion. My own is that he is not. His goodness of intention is too pure, his nobility too exalted, and his emotions too uncomplicated. Perhaps, of course, such a criticism applied to a play written for the stage is unfair, but the same criticism can be made (as will be seen) of the heroes of Bird's novels. In each of them, even in Spartacus, there is a vein of weakness usually arising out of a super-refined sense of honor. In the case of *The Gladiator*, however, the impression of Spartacus' character as unrealistic perhaps arises even more out of the orotund speeches that he delivers. However splendid the rhetoric may have been in the mouth of Forrest and however mellifluous Bird's blank verse seemed to his contemporaries, a modern critic must divest himself of many prejudices before he can see much more than rant in Bird's style. There are good passages. That in which Spartacus describes the ravage by the Romans of his Thracian homeland to the centurion Jovius has been praised by all the critics, and the following speech by Spartacus is an example of Bird's flowing blank verse and high sentiment at its best:

> Well, I am here,
> Among these beasts of Rome, a spectacle.
> This is the temple, where they mock the Gods
> With human butchery,—Most grand and glorious
> Of structure and device!—It should have been a cave,
> Some foul and midnight pit, or den of bones,
> Where murder best might veil himself from sight.—
> Women and children, too, to see men die,
> And clap their hands at every stab! This is
> The boastful excellence of Rome! I thank the Gods
> There are Barbarians.
> (Act II, Scene iii)

But in general the style is stilted, turgid, unnatural, and derivative. This is an example of a conversation between the consul Crassus and Florus, suitor to his niece:

> CRASSUS
>
> What, Sirrah, again? Hast thou not had thy answer?
> Kill me these flies that being lean themselves,
> Swarm after fatness. Why art thou this fool,
> To covet my rich niece?
>
> FLORUS
> I seek not riches.
>
> CRASSUS
>
> Pah! Will poor lovers sing eternally
> The self-same song? They seek not riches! Jove,
> Why pass they then all poverty, where their choice
> Might find a wider compass?
> (Act II, Scene i)

Such foolish pseudo-Shakespearean language is not, of course, the fault of Bird alone: he was writing in the tragic style of his time. But, despite the frequent rhetorical skill and real beauties of his tragic writing, today most of it seems unreal and strained.

CHAPTER 5

South American Plays

IN HIS last two major plays Bird turned from Rome and Greece
to South America for his background. In doing so, while still
retaining the advantages of a distant and romantic locale, he
followed the current trend toward American rather than European
subjects. He was also following the great revival of interest in
Spanish and Spanish American subjects stimulated by Washington Irving's histories and sketches of Columbus and of the
conquistadores.

Just as *Pelopidas* and *The Gladiator* take their places in a long
tradition of plays on classical subjects, so Bird's *Oralloossa, Son
of the Incas* is part of an even more sharply defined fashion in
America of Indian plays.[1] As early as 1766 Robert Rogers of
Rogers' Rangers fame had written a play (never performed)
entitled *Ponteach, or The Savages of America*; and in 1794, under
the sponsorship of the Tammany Society, Anne Kemble had
staged an unsuccessful operatic extravaganza called *Tammany*.
James N. Barker's *The Indian Princess; or, La Belle Sauvage*
(1808) was the first of a long series of plays on the Pocahontas
theme. Great popularity came to the Indian drama with George
Washington Parke Custis' *The Indian Prophecy* (1827) and
Pocahontas, or The Settlers of Virginia (1830). At least two of
the early Indian plays, both produced in 1800, had been set in
Peru: William Dunlap's version of Kotzebue's *The Virgin of the
Sun* and the sequel, *Pizarro in Peru, or The Death of Rolla*.
The character of Rolla, nature's nobleman, in the latter play was
one of Forrest's great roles.

But the vogue was really set by Forrest's vigorous and repeated
performances in Stone's bombastic *Metamora* (1829), which
became the Indian play beyond all others and had a host of rivals
and imitators. Indeed, between 1825 and 1860 the stage was

assailed by at least forty highly romanticized and statuesque Indian braves and maidens with such euphonious names as Sassacus, Kairissah, Outalassie, Onylda, Ontiata, Osceola, Oronooka, Tuscalomba, Carabasset, and Hiawatha. Some of the authors of these aboriginal dramas were Robert Dale Owen, Charlotte M. S. Barnes, Lewis Deffebach, Nathaniel Deering, Joseph Doddridge, and William Emmons. By 1846, as James Rees remarks, the Indian plays had become a perfect nuisance. Fortunately the fashion was finally laughed out of existence by a couple of clever burlesques by John Brougham in *Metamora; or The Last of the Pollywoags* (1847) and in a popular work with the resounding title *An Original Aboriginal Erratic Operatic Semi-Civilized and Demi-Savage Extravaganza, being a Per-Version of Ye Trewe and Wonderfull Hystorie of a Rennowned Princess Pocahontas; or The Gentle Savage* (1855).[2]

Interested in Indians as he was throughout his life, Bird as dramatist could hardly have failed to make his contribution to this dramatic vogue. As we have seen, he very early planned a play on King Philip. Now, perhaps at the suggestion of Forrest, who had made such a success in *Metamora*, he wrote *Oralloossa*. Later, in 1836, at the request of Forrest he made a complete revision, indeed a rewriting, of Stone's *Metamora*. Forrest wanted the manuscript of this revision for his tour to England; but when later asked to pay Bird for making it, he refused on the grounds that he had never used it. Unfortunately Bird had made no copy, since at the time of his writing he was busy revising proofs of *Calavar*. In 1856 Bird's brother-in-law Edward Mayer tried to get Forrest to return the manuscript to the Bird family, but Forrest said that he had misplaced it and did not know where it was. It is still missing. Among Bird's papers, however, are a number of fragments and plans which seem to support Mary Bird's assertion that it was really a new play altogether, for the plot, construction, incidents, characters, and language are wholly different from Stone's.

I *Oralloossa, Son of the Incas*

Bird's tragedy of the Spanish conquest of Peru involves the struggle for power not only between Indian and Spaniard but also, on the Spanish side, between Pizarro and young Almagro and, on the Indian side, between the rightful Inca Oralloossa and the usurping Inca Manco. Disguised as a servant, Oralloossa wins the confidence of Pizarro and persuades him to destroy Almagro and his followers at a banquet. At the same time he arranges matters so that at the same banquet Almagro plans to kill Pizarro. Oralloossa, in turn, intends to see that all the Spaniards are slain. Although Pizarro is killed, Almagro through the love of Ooallie, Oralloossa's beautiful sister, survives to double-cross Oralloossa with the help of Manco. Oralloossa and Ooallie are dragged off to prison, from which the former escapes. Enraged at Manco, he betrays the Indian cause by leading the new viceroy De Castro against Manco and Almagro. Ooallie, who has been buried alive, dies after the priest who was to have rescued her is killed. Oralloossa kills Almagro in a striking cavern scene (Bird loved caves!) and then dies. All hope for resistance against the Spaniards is over.

In October, 1832, Edwin Forrest produced *Oralloossa, Son of the Incas* in a magnificent production in Philadelphia. He provided new costumes, banners, and properties. Coyle and Leslie, two of the best scene painters in America, painted twelve splendid panoramic scenes with geographically accurate views of the Peruvian Andes. Especially effective was the scene for Act IV of the Peruvian camp in which the Peruvian hosts picturesquely swarm over the whole landscape from the plain high up toward the Andes. The scene in Pizarro's banquet hall was magnificent and that in the recesses of the gigantic cavern, a masterpiece of scenic art. For five nights, despite the competition of the Kembles playing at another theater in Philadelphia, *Oralloossa* drew large crowds. Only one mishap took place. Forrest, playing Oralloossa, lunged so fiercely at F. C. Wemyss as Don Christobal that Wemyss lost two of his front teeth—an event which may explain Wemyss's particular dislike of the play. The reviews both in Philadelphia and elsewhere were laudatory. One Philadelphia reviewer called it a "most brilliant and triumphal success"; in Boston also it was termed "brilliantly successful."

But there was disappointment too. After the tremendous effect of *The Gladiator*, audiences expected something even more spectacular. The poetry of *Oralloossa* was not so striking as that of its predecessor, and the play lacked the drums and trumpets and the high rhetoric about battling for freedom that had made the earlier play so effective. Again there was criticism that the climax came too early. After the powerful banquet scene in which, following the quarrel between Almagro and Pizarro, the no longer disguised Oralloossa enters in his true character as Inca and kills Pizarro, the interest of the play wanes. Though the young hero Oralloossa is noble and attractive, the critics said, the play lacks incident, and the dialogue seems stiff. On such grounds both Rees and Wemyss call the play a failure. It is certainly true that, though he kept it in his repertoire until as late as 1847, Forrest did not play it regularly after its first run. The truth is probably that *Oralloossa* depended to a greater extent than *The Gladiator* on the *mise en scène*. It won its applause largely as a brilliant, colorful historical pageant something akin to the panorama shows that were becoming popular in the America of the day. As such, depending on brilliant costume and striking scenery, it was costly to stage. No doubt the expense was one of the reasons that Forrest gradually withdrew it.

Despite some fine set speeches and some effective scenes like the death of Pizarro, the betrayal of Oralloossa, and the scene in which Oralloossa is accused of madness by Manco and Almagro, *Oralloossa* is not an effective play. Writing (as he said) with more care than in *The Gladiator* and with more attention to common sense,[3] Bird is restricted perhaps too much by his numerous historical sources. Yet at the same time he creates in Oralloossa an entirely unhistorical figure, not only in the fact that no such Inca ever really existed but also in that a sixteenth-century barbarian is given (as was the Roman slave Spartacus) sentiments of chivalry and patriotic ideals of liberty characteristic only of the nineteenth century. Such overemphasis on historical accuracy on the one hand and yet tampering with history on the other would certainly be pardonable were the result a successful and appealing play. But *Oralloossa* is not. The dramatic fiction that an Inca could live for months or years as the confidential slave of Almagro and Pizarro is ridiculous. The play is slow-moving, and there are too many and too complicated plots, with both the Spaniards and the Peruvians divided into struggling factions. The climax, as the critics said, does come too early—whether one sees it in the death of Pizarro or in the failure of Oralloossa's hopes and in his and his sister's imprisonment. The last act is both thoroughly confused and without a center of interest. And

Oralloossa's final revenge against Almagro has not sufficient importance or meaning to provide a strong conclusion.

Furthermore, the play suffers from the weakness of almost all plays and novels on Aztec or Inca subjects. On the one hand, we are asked to sympathize with Peruvian Indians fighting for their freedom. But, on the other, Bird, like other authors, cannot forget that the Indians are barbarians and that the Spaniards are Christians. Thus we are asked to feel for the noble Oralloossa and yet also to sympathize with Spaniards who betray him because he is Indian. The entrance of Vaca de Castro at the end, though it supposedly sets all right, is really the death-seal on Peruvian hopes for liberation. As a result there are few characters or causes in the play with which we can become emotionally involved. The Spaniards are thoroughly despicable, though we can admire the forcefulness of Pizarro: Almagro is a traitor; Christobal, though supposedly honorable and good, is untrue to Ooallie and the Indians. Even Oralloossa is too wily to be a strong national hero. As Pedro he worms his way into the confidence of Almagro only to betray him to Pizarro; then he betrays Pizarro to his death; and, when the Peruvians turn against him, he tries to betray them to the Spaniards. His motive in trusting Almagro—he trusts him because his sister loves him—is weak.

Bird said that his purpose in the play was "first, the portraiture of a barbarian in which is concentered all those qualities both of good and evil which are most strikingly characteristic of savage life; the second, to show how the noblest designs of a great man and the brightest destinies of a nation could be interrupted and destroyed by the unprincipled ambition of a single individual."[4] But Bird cannot accept Oralloossa as truly "great" for the very reason that he is in some respects typically "savage" (though in other respects unhistorically sentimental). More important, Bird's eye is so obviously on historical or moral questions that he forgets to create a truly strong hero.

II *The Broker of Bogota*

In what many critics consider his finest play, Bird turned from heroic to domestic drama. The scene, which could have been placed anywhere, is Santa Fe de Bogota in New Granada. *The Broker of Bogota*, written for Forrest and first played on January

12, 1834, concerns a middle-class moneylender Febro, his wild but penitent son Ramon, his good son Francisco, and his daughter Leonor, who is in love with Fernando, son of the Viceroy. The villain of the piece is Cabarero, a decayed nobleman who has led Ramon into profligacy and debt. Disowned by his father and rejected as a suitor by the father of Juana, the girl whom he loves, Ramon is led by Cabarero into a plot to steal a large sum of money that the Viceroy has deposited in Febro's vault. Just as, unknown to Ramon, his father is beginning to relent, the robbery is carried out in such a way as to make it seem that Febro himself is involved. Brought before the Viceroy, Febro in his grief and bewilderment cannot defend himself, and, though he pleads with Ramon to clear him, Ramon is too weak to confess his own part in the crime. Febro is further struck down by the news that his daughter Leonor has secretly eloped with an unknown suitor. In the end, through Juana's efforts Febro's innocence and Ramon's guilt become apparent, and Leonor's lover is found to be the Viceroy's own son. But for Febro and Ramon it is too late: Ramon kills himself; Febro dies.

After the first performance of *The Broker*, Forrest enthusiastically wrote to Bird: "I have just left the theater—your tragedy was performed and crowned with entire success. *The Broker of Bogota* will live when our vile trunks are rotten." Though this prediction was perhaps over-optimistic, Forrest himself did keep the play in his repertoire and played it for many years.

Since then the play has certainly been often praised. Rees thinks it superior to all American plays as *King Lear* is to all British plays.[5] Quinn, with his usual enthusiasm, calls Cabarero "one of the finest villains of the stage" and has emphasized the great appeal of the play's "fidelity to human nature."[6] William R. Alger, the biographer of Edwin Forrest, says that it is "a naked, simple drama of real life in its familiar course."[7]

These comments are obviously extreme. While we need not agree with Sydney George Fisher, who on seeing Forrest in the play in 1837 wrote in his diary that it was a bad play, full of false feeling, absurd situations, and with a wretched and unnatural plot,[8] or with Margaret Mayorga, who dismisses it as dealing merely with the smaller emotions of the life of a miser,[9] we must admit that it is melodramatic. The life pictured in it is assuredly not "life in its familiar course," nor is the drama "naked and

simple." Indeed, the plot is highly complicated. It is true, however, that in turning away from the heroic and national drama
toward drama concerned with middle-class life, Bird was slightly
in advance of his time in America. But whether the great appeal
of *The Broker* really lies in its "fidelity to human nature" is
another matter, since the situations and characters are not those
of real life, and the events and emotional reactions are all
exaggerated. It is certainly not true that the deviltry of Cabarero
is never overemphasized, as Quinn states. Though Cabarero is
an effective scoundrel and though Bird gives him adequate
motives for his villainy, he assuredly belongs to the subtle,
moustache-twisting, devilish legion of villains who plagued the
nineteenth-century theater.

On the other hand, the play does have strong merits and, as
Arthur Hornblow states, probably is the drama of Bird's with the
most literary finish.[10] But there are weaknesses in the plot. For
example, it seems entirely too coincidental that just as Cabarero
has brought Ramon to the highest pitch of anger against his
father Febro, Ramon should find the lost key to the vault.
(Possibly, of course, Cabarero has found it earlier and places
it now in Ramon's way.) The subplot involving the love of
Fernando and Leonor is also weak, because no motivation is given
for Fernando's concealing his identity as the Viceroy's son from
Leonor, nor is there any reason for him to invent the story of a
quarrel between Febro and his father when they are actually
good friends. If this were not a play, he would of course let
Leonor into the secret of who he really is. But in general the plot
is clever. Every circumstance, whether planned by the devilish
Cabarero or happening through other causes, is so contrived as
to tighten more securely the entanglement of seeming guilt around
Febro's innocence. Both the trial scene, which is like one from a
modern detective play, and the scene in which Febro, cleared
of guilt, tries to argue that his son Ramon is also innocent are,
though melodramatic, highly effective in reading and would be
more so on the stage.

Bird's most important advance over the earlier plays, however,
is in the relationship between action and characterization. Much
more than in the other plays what happens is based on the traits
of the characters. Bird has also learned how to create strong
minor characters who enhance rather than detract from the main

characters. Juana's skill in tricking Ramon into confessing his part in the robbery, for instance, makes her a real person but at the same time contributes to the basically more important theme, the character of Ramon. Furthermore, the central tragedy arises logically out of the foolish pride of both father and son. Though penitent, Ramon will not humble himself to Febro; and Febro, though longing to reclaim his first-born, will not forgive him until he has humbled himself. Cabarero, of course, strives incessantly to put difficulties in the way of a reconciliation, but in an important sense Cabarero can really be considered almost an objectified aspect of Ramon's character. With all the characters except Cabarero we can have great sympathy, foolish and wrong though their actions may be. In the end, when too late the Viceroy sets all straight, we have a feeling of warmth and pity that is entirely lacking in the cold conclusion of *Oralloossa* or even the gallant heroics of *The Gladiator*. Though not his most popular play, in many ways Bird's last drama is his best. It was his own favorite.

III *From Drama to Fiction*

At the very height of his reputation as a dramatist Robert Montgomery Bird stopped writing plays. In part, this was the result of a long settled plan: in charting out his future literary course in 1828 Bird had determined at some point in his career to turn from dramatic writing to fiction, just as he had planned to turn in later years from fiction to history. But also his determination to write no more plays was partly caused by a disgust with the theater and the life of a playwright. He was tired of being a playwright. He felt himself—and any ordinary man— inadequate to the demands playwrighting made. "What a fool I was," he wrote in his *Secret Records* early in his career, "to think of writing plays! To be sure, they are much wanted. But then novels are much easier sorts of things and immortalize one's pocket much sooner. A tragedy takes, or should take, as much labour as two romances; and one comedy as much as six tragedies." And what was the reward of the dramatist? It was "to be chronicled with such fellows as Sheil, and Knowles, and Payne, and Peake—How monosyllabic we dramatists be! But our genius is as diminutive as our names."[11]

A play, Bird thought, ran many more risks than a romance.

After a novel was completed, it did not have to go through the fiery furnace of theatrical production nor suffer from the ignorance and incompetence of actors. The average theatrical company, Bird had discovered to his disgust, had only two or three good actors, and thus the dramatist had to fashion his play so that it depended almost wholly on two or three parts.[12] "In fine" (as Foust summarizes the passage), "considering the oblivion, the shabby returns, the risks and difficulties, the exacting and varying requirements that lie in the way of the dramatist, 'it is not wonderful few men have the courage to tread it. The marvel is that any are found so daring.' "[13] Turning aside, then, from what he considered a higher though more arduous career of dramatist, Bird now took the easier path of a writer of novels.

But these theoretical views tell only part of the story of Bird's break with drama; his resolution to have nothing more to do with the theater was actually a result of his dealings with Edwin Forrest. Bird abandoned playwrighting because he felt that he was being cheated and because he had found that, as a result of the lack of copyright protection, he could not make a fair living as a dramatist.

Forrest, it will be remembered, had offered prizes of one thousand dollars each for dramas by Americans. Bird had written four prize-winning plays: *Pelopidas, The Gladiator, Oralloossa,* and *The Broker of Bogota.* Because *The Gladiator* had been substituted for *Pelopidas,* nothing had been paid for the latter, but Forrest had paid the thousand dollars for each of the other three. Since he also had advanced two thousand dollars to Bird as a loan, Forrest thought that Bird was two thousand dollars in debt to him. But Bird's understanding of the situation was far different. He had understood that for each of the plays, if it were successful, he was to receive three thousand dollars; and he asserted also that Forrest owed him two thousand dollars for the revisions of *Metamora* which he had commissioned him to make. Hence according to Bird, the balance stood the other way: Forrest, having paid only five thousand of eleven thousand dollars, still owed Bird six thousand dollars. The plays had been successful. From *The Gladiator* alone Forrest had made tens of thousands of dollars; indeed, he had made a large fortune from the plays of Bird and other authors to whom he had paid only pittances.

All this misunderstanding came out in the open when in 1837—probably because of his marriage and the prompting of his bride (who had a much better business head than had Bird himself)—Bird tried to come to a settlement with Forrest. They met in Bird's house; there was violent disagreement; the once good friends parted never to meet again. Forrest refused even to return to Bird the manuscript revisions for *Metamora,* which he asserted he had never used, and he persisted in this refusal to the end of his life. Nor would he permit Bird or his heirs to publish any of the plays, claiming exclusive rights over them and asserting (falsely, as it long afterwards developed) that he had copyrighted them in his own name. Bird was left helpless in the matter. Always a trusting person who believed everyone to be as honest as himself, and having been at the time on the best of terms with Forrest, he had neglected to secure a written contract. When in 1851 he considered bringing suit, the witnesses to the oral agreement were dead. Neither he nor his heirs after him could ever obtain justice from Forrest. From that time he wrote no more for the theater (though he revised his plays in a vain hope of publication), and he attended hardly a play. Thoroughly disgusted, he turned to the novel.

Yet for all the injustice to Bird, Forrest cannot be wholly condemned. He was merely following the custom of his time in the theater, buying his plays as cheaply as he could, taking the risk of their failure, and keeping their manuscripts in his own hands to prevent their being stolen and used by competing actors. Without Forrest, and indeed without Forrest's revisions, Bird's plays would doubtless have either not been written at all or would have remained locked in their author's portfolio. What was needed, of course, was a strong law of dramatic copyright, a law the passage of which Bird later used all his political influence to promote. He planned an article on the matter entitled "Dramatic Authors and Their Profits," telling the whole story and accusing Forrest of having cheated John Augustus Stone so badly that Stone eventually committed suicide. And long afterwards, in 1853, he wrote the dramatist George Boker—who was attempting to push a dramatic copyright bill through Congress—strongly supporting his campaign and saying that, if such a law had been in force twenty years earlier, he would never have abandoned playwrighting.

CHAPTER 6

Romances of Mexico

AS A NOVELIST, Robert Montgomery Bird continued in very much the same paths that he had followed as dramatist: the practised playwright often shows under the romancer. In the novels much of the dialogue is close to that of the stage, and incidents in the novels are often managed as if with an eye to scenic effect. The three main kinds of novels which Bird wrote—historical romances of the conquest of Mexico, romances of backwoodsmen and Indians, and novels of satire on American life—are all foreshadowed in his comedies and tragedies. The ease with which *Nick of the Woods* and *The Infidel* were turned into successful stage plays is further evidence of how close their plotting and rhetoric where to the drama of the day. Many of the specific subjects which Bird had first planned to use for plays were later used, or planned for use, in the novels and short tales.

With his usual optimistic industry, Bird again and again drew up long lists of projected novels. In one of these he lists over thirty novels already written or to be written. Of these he wrote (if we consider the fragmentary *A Belated Revenge* a novel) only seven. But these seven illustrate very clearly the three main types of novel or romance which he contemplated. They also clearly place him as a novelist in three or four important traditions of early nineteenth-century American fiction.

Calavar; or, The Knight of the Conquest, A Romance of Mexico and *The Infidel; or, The Fall of Mexico* are romances of exotic history in the tradition first popularized by Sir Walter Scott in *Ivanhoe* and *The Talisman* and carried on by Bulwer in *The Last Days of Pompeii,* and in America by Cooper in *The Bravo, The Heidenmauer,* and *Mercedes of Castile.* Within this tradition Bird's novels inaugurate a long series dealing with the Aztecs and Incas and the early history of Spanish America. In them (as he had already in *Oralloossa*) Bird faced the difficulties which all later authors encountered in treating the Spanish conquest. Undaunted, however, he at various times planned at least eight novels on Mexico and Peru. In one general series of "Legends of the New World," which he evidently thought of publishing in England, the second of the three series was to have consisted of three "Tales of Mexico," one about the invasion, one set during the vice-royalty, and one about the Mexican Revolution. the third series was to consist of tales of Peru (probably the same tales in prose that he had once planned as poems in his projected book *El Dorado*). At other times he planned a novel *Fedalla, A Tale of Peru* (perhaps the same as another projected novel with the title *Stephen of Leon, A Tale of Peru*); the plot, laid in Peru at the time of Pizarro, sounds very much like a revision of the material of *Oralloossa* into the form of a romance. He actually wrote some chapters of *The Volunteers, A Tale of "The Times That Tried Men Souls,"* a novel about the Mexican war, the purpose of which was to show the bravery of the American volunteers at Buena Vista and other battles.[1]

I *Calavar*

Calavar tells the story of the first phase of the Spanish conquest of Mexico. After Cortez has garrisoned the capital city Tenochtitlan (Mexico City), Narvaez is sent by the governor to replace him, but Cortez defeats the new general at Zempoala. With the troops of both armies Cortez returns to Tenochtitlan, where he has to contend now with strong opposition from the Mexicans. Spaniards and Indians fight in the streets and on the temple pyramids; the emperor Montezuma, imprisoned by the Spaniards, is killed by his own rebel subjects; the Spaniards are besieged and starved until they have no choice but to retreat at night over one of the causeways, thereby incurring the deadly massacre of the *Noche Triste;* yet faced with impossible numerical odds they defeat the Mexican armies at the battle of Otumba.

Intertwined with the historical narrative is the tale of the half-mad Knight of St. John, Calavar, and his young and noble nephew Amador. Calavar, driven to distraction by the weight of guilt incurred by his betrayal of a noble Moorish friend and a beloved

Moorish girl during the wars against the Moors in Spain, has come to expiate his sins in battles against the pagan Mexicans. On his way to join his uncle, Amador, also torn by remorse because he has lost sight of the lovely damsel whom he loves, picks up at sea a mysterious Moor named Abdalla and his graceful young "son" Jacinto. In Mexico Jacinto first becomes page to Calavar but is then spirited away by Abdalla, who has joined the Mexicans against the Spaniards. Jacinto is made to act the part of a pagan goddess. In the long explanation at the end of the book Abdalla is revealed as the noble Moor whom Calavar thought he had betrayed to death many years before; Jacinto is revealed to be the lovely daughter of Calavar's beloved (whom he thought he had killed in a burst of jealous rage) and also the damsel whom Amador had loved and lost in Spain. Of course, though for months she has acted as his and his uncle's page, he has not recognized her! Calavar, chastened but sane, dies after performing miraculous feats of valor at the battle of Otumba, but Amador and the girl Leila (who is really a Christian) are married and can start life anew.

When *Calavar* was published in 1834, it was hailed in the almost unanimously favorable reviews as opening up a new geographical and historical area for the American novelist. Irving had already published his histories of Columbus and the early Spanish explorers, but Prescott had not yet written his *Conquest of Mexico*. Because of the recent revolutions in Spanish America, there was much current interest in that region. Bird pioneered in capitalizing on that interest. He had found a subject which, while still being American, had all the strangeness and exotic qualities of Old World romance. He was thus rightly hailed for treading "untrodden ground"[2] long overlooked and for providing "a new field for romance."[3]

If for no other reason, *Calavar* is valuable as an exciting and accurate narrative of history. Bird himself wrote in the preface to the edition of 1847 that his chief purpose in the novel had been to illustrate what he considered the most romantic and poetical chapter in the history of the New World. Indeed, the novel had been meant merely to prepare the way for a projected history of Mexico. Thus he had "written with an attempt at the strictest historical accuracy compatible with the requisitions of romance."

Bird had, of course, been long interested in Spanish America. With his tireless energy for research he had studied hard and long the history, geography, and people of the region. Pages and pages of notes in his notebooks testify to his scholarly zeal. James Rees thought that he was "more familiar with the history of South America, and Spanish North America, than any other man in the country." The result was that in the novel he tells his story from the best original sources (he read Spanish fluently), and most of his facts and historical conclusions can be relied upon. Prescott, in a note to the *History of the Conquest of Mexico,* testified to Bird's historical accuracy. Commenting on Bird's account of the *mantas,* or movable towers, which Cortez constructed to dislodge the Mexicans from their high buildings, Prescott remarked:

> Dr. Bird, in his picturesque romance of "Calavar," has made good use of these *mantas,* better, indeed, than can be permitted to the historian. He claims the privilege of the romancer; though it must be owned he does not abuse this privilege, for he has studied with great care the costume, manners, and military usages of the natives. He has done for them what Cooper has done for the wild tribes of the North,—touched their rude features with the bright coloring of a poetic fancy. He has been equally fortunate in his delineation of the picturesque scenery of the land. If he has been less so in attempting to revive the antique dialogue of the Spanish cavalier, we must not be surprised. Nothing is more difficult than the skilful execution of a modern antique. It requires all the genius and learning of Scott to execute it so that the connoisseur shall not detect the counterfeit.[4]

Much, indeed, of the merit of *Calavar* and *The Infidel* lies in the vividness of their pictures of the thrilling scenes of battle and massacre. Though, as Prescott intimates, the dialogue of the Spanish cavaliers and indeed the whole vocabulary of the novels is atrociously stilted and fantastically inflated and long-winded, the descriptions of action are excellent. Poe was right when he said that Bird excelled in the drama of action.[5] We do not soon forget the battle between Cortez and Narvaez by the pyramid of Cholula, the fights in the streets of Tenochtitlan, the siege of the Spaniards in Montezuma's palace, or the bloody massacre of the *Noche Triste*. When they are in action, the

characters, especially the historical ones, are vivid and convincing. Bird, the former dramatist, is also skillful at creating
striking scenic effects. The death of Montezuma, the appearance
of Leila as a pagan prophetess, and the ghostly appearance
of Calavar at Otumba are well conceived; they remind one of
the best pageantry of *The Gladiator* or *Oralloossa*. Furthermore,
as Prescott says, Bird is excellent in many of his set descriptions
of scenery. For one who had never been to Mexico, he is
remarkable in his ability to bring before us the beauty and
character of the Mexican landscape, both as it now is and as
he imagines it to have been at the advent of the Spaniards.
We wonder, indeed, whether he had not seen Buller's or some
other panorama of Mexico, ancient and modern, since his
best set pieces are just those that a skilled panoramist would
have painted.

To his vivid epic of the conquest of a great empire, Bird
unfortunately adds an impossibly intricate fictional plot. In
Calavar it is the story of the Knight of St. John, his nephew
Amador, his rival now disguised as Abdalla the Moor, and the
beautiful page Jacinto. With great, perhaps too great ingenuity
Bird weaves a complicated web of circumstances in which the
characters are caught. At the end, in several pages of explanation, the web is finally unravelled and the circumstances
explained. But the reader really does not care. Like the foolish
hocus-pocus of the conjuror Botello (actually an historical
character), the Gothic melodrama of the half-mad knight
Byronically mourning because he has loved and killed, the
undying vengeance of the Moor, and the vicissitudes of virtue
of the maiden dressed as a boy only detract from the vigor of
the historical narrative. There are too many coincidences and
absurdities for us to believe. That Don Amador should by chance
fall in love with the daughter of his uncle's beloved, that Abdalla
(the uncle's former friend and rival whom he thought he had
slain) should by chance be picked up and brought to Mexico,
that Don Amador would not recognize his beloved Leila though
continuously with her for days at a time–these are the conventions of the romance of the time, but they detract from the real
story. So too do the midnight visions of the dead, the incessant
moaning of Calavar over his guilt, and the too-noble loyalty of
Don Amador to his kinsman. Calavar's escape from the massacre

is also not convincingly explained. We wish here (as we do in other of Bird's novels and also in many of the novels of Cooper and Scott) that the whole romantic plot and its fictional characters could have been omitted and that an historical character, such as Cortez or one of his cavaliers or even the Moor, had been made the hero. As it is, the historical characters are much stronger than the purely fictional ones. At least, they do not go into trances, swoon, weep, and carry on so foolishly as the fictional characters too often do.

Perhaps even more damaging to the novel, as an excellent review in the *American Monthly Magazine* (December, 1834) pointed out, is the fact that Bird has left his novel with no real hero or heroine. Though we hear of their adventures, we know too little about the real personalities of Calavar and Amador to have any true feeling for them. About the female characters we know even less. Had Jacinto, this reviewer remarks, only been brought on the scene earlier in her true character, we might have learned something of her reactions to her difficult situation and thus have sympathized with her. But, in the interest of a surprise that is not really a surprise to the reader, Bird loses the fertile psychological situation and reveals the "boy" as Leila only at the hurried, final unravelling of his story. In human terms, then, the story has no progression, and the end is unsatisfactorily mechanical. The novel, which had great potentialities for the development of characters, remains a thin tissue of historical fact and gorgeous description.

That the style of *Calavar* is stilted and awkward Bird himself admitted in his preface to the "new edition" of 1847. For the new edition he really should, he says, have condensed the lengthy dialogues, lightened the heavy descriptions, and modernized the antiquated phraseology. The modern critic must certainly agree with Bird's own criticism and regret that Bird did not find the time to revise. Yet, though much of the style is ridiculously mannered and archaic, in time we almost grow used to it and begin to enjoy it.

Another major weakness, however, is less easy to ignore. This further fault *Calavar* shares with almost the whole long series of novels and poems of the Spanish conquests of Mexico and Peru that followed Bird's two novels. *Oralloossa* had been weakened by it; even Prescott's splendid histories suffer because of it; and we find it also to some extent in Cooper's novels of northern Indians. The fault is ambivalence in values. On the one hand, Bird and the other authors conceive of the Aztecs and Incas as nature's noblemen, living in a civilization to some extent superior to that of the Spaniards. They are patriots laudably defending their homelands, their wives and children and sacred altars, from the fierce, cruel, rapacious, untrustworthy invaders. Obviously the reader must sympathize with them. Yet, on the other hand, they are barbarian savages, and the Spaniards are white "civilized" men. Even more important is the fact that the Spaniards are Christians while the Aztecs, at least, were given to gory human sacrifice. The author could not, in the nineteenth century, take as his hero a pagan who kills Christians and does not suffer for it. Nor could he have a Christian hero who joined with pagans against other Christians. Though his character might sympathize with them, though he might act with them to a certain point, though he might even be in love with a beautiful (Christian or naturally pious) Indian maiden—at the crucial moment religion and color and race must tell, with the result that he must rejoin his Christian comrades in their work of devastation and ravage. Various authors after Bird tried to solve the problem cleverly. Henty, in *By Right of Conquest,* made the hero an English Protestant who can thus see both Spaniards and Indians as evil in their ways. In Fosdick's *Malmiztic the Toltec,* the hero is an Indian of a good and virtuous tribe who, like the English Protestant, can rejoice in the calamities of both Spaniard and Aztec.

Bird, however, like the vast majority of authors on the subject, developed no such clever solution and was therefore confronted with a dilemma of sympathy. Throughout the early parts of *Calavar* he repeatedly uses the symbol of Eden; he was one of the first American novelists to use that symbol which was to be so important in American fiction. The beautiful Tenochtitlan of the Aztecs, surrounded by its lovely lake, its gardens, its fertile fields, and its tributary kingdoms, is compared to the Garden of Eden; Cortez is the Miltonic Satan looking over the wall and half-regretting that his ambition must cause him to destroy the beauty that he sees there. In his account of the terrible calamity of the *Noche Triste,* while he is describing the Mexicans' slaying of the Spaniards who are attempting to retreat across the causeway, Bird remarks that the massacre was "the dreadful punishment of men who acknowledged no rights but those of power, and preferred to rob a weak and childish race with insult and murder, rather than to subdue them, as could have been done, by the arts of peace." Yet in every crucial moment Bird is strongly on the Spanish side. Calavar, who by implication is repeating his sin of destroying the noble Moors in Spain, fights for Cortez and indeed wins for the Spaniards the battle of Otumba. Amador, though he has the chance to remain neutral when he lies wounded in the Aztec house of Abdalla and Leila, rises at the risk of his life to fight with the Spaniards. The Moor, for whom Bird often shows much sympathy because of his wrongs in Spain, is branded as a renegade to his race when he quite naturally joins with the Mexicans in seeking to destroy the Spaniards. Bird, like the other authors, does not quite know on which side he really should be. In a history such balancing of values might perhaps be justified (though in his highly dramatic narrative even Prescott is annoying in his contradictory sympathies). In a novel it means that the author is able really to say very little. Perhaps this difficulty is the main reason why, though the basic material of the Spanish conquest seems ideally suited for romance, so few novels of any real quality during the nineteenth century were based on it.

II *The Infidel*

In *The Infidel* this ambivalence is even more pronounced. The narrative here, equally or indeed more pretentiously historical, carries the story of the conquest through Cortez' preparations to besiege the Mexican capital, the siege itself, the heroic defense of the Aztec King Guatimozin, and the final victory of the Spaniards and utter destruction of the city. The fictional subplot has as its main characters Juan Lerma, a former favorite of Cortez, now in deadly disfavor; Magdalena or Infeliz, a former nun with whom Juan had been in love but whom he now spurns since he thinks her the mistress of Cortez; Camarga, a Dominican friar, who turns out in the very complicated explanation at the end to be the father of both Juan and Infeliz; and Zelahualla, the daughter of Montezuma, whom Juan finally marries and happily carries back to Spain. Juan Lerma himself, whom the villain Guzman has pictured to Cortez as the lover of Cortez' wife and whom the general has therefore tried to kill by sending on extraordinarily dangerous missions, turns out to be Cortez' own nephew; he finally gains Cortez' favor and regains the estates in Spain that have been perfidiously withheld from him.

Many of the incidents of this exceedingly intricate plot are striking. In a suspenseful scene Cortez tears up the paper on which are listed the names of the Spaniards who have conspired against him. Infeliz tries to rescue Juan from the dungeon in which he is confined under sentence of death. Guatimozin, true emperor of Mexico, comes in disguise into the midst of his Spanish foes and spirits Juan away just in time to save him from death. Cortez' small sailing ships, carried with infinite labor up to the lake, battle the swarms of native canoes. Famine horribly reduces the besieged Indian capital Tenochtitlan to pathetic agony. Guzman, villain though he is, one foot bound, heroically battles the Indian warriors in the ceremony of the stone of sacrifice until at the climactic moment Juan intervenes to try to save him. Many of the Mexicans, despite their barbarously unpronounceable names, are noble and brave; many of the Spaniards are colorfully evil.

Yet from the very start of the novel the conflict in Bird's sympathies is evident. The Spaniards are praised as "unconquerable" and "capable of every expedient." The whites are "a nobler race" than the Indians. Yet at the same time Juan, the hero, disapproves of the Spaniards' cruelty and treachery, and in Chaper XVII of Volume I occurs the speech of the Mexican ambassador to Cortez in which he convincingly argues that the Indians are fighting courageously, patriotically, and honorably against a perfidious foe. The ambassador is compared to a noble Spartan bravely speaking his message at the court of the Persians. Juan's own loyalties are unbelievably confused. He is in love with an Indian girl; he is friendly with Guatimozin, emperor of Mexico; yet, even though he is to be hanged the next day by Cortez, he is angry at Guatimozin's kidnapping him to save his life. He tries desperately to escape from the Mexicans in order to return to the Spaniards—to be hanged! Though condemned to death by them, he will not be a traitor to the

Spaniards. But, on the fallacious plea that he will stop bloodshed by assisting the Spanish conquest, he thinks it right in the circumstances to betray the confidence that Guatimozin, who has saved his life, has placed in him. When his worst enemy, he who has slandered him and caused all his troubles with Cortez, is about to die at the hands of the Mexicans in the amphitheater scene, Juan, breaking his parole, intervenes to save him because he cannot see a Spaniard die at the hands of the Mexicans. Indians, of course, fall by multitudes, but the only real sympathy Bird shows is for the Spaniards. Toward the end the patriotic Guatimozin is described as only a stubborn "infidel"; and the Mexican empire falls at the hand of God because of its atrocious human sacrifices. Yet earlier we had been convinced that the stuggle of Guatimozin was a noble fight for country and liberty. Bird is confused between his romantic sympathy for the Mexicans, his desire for a noble European hero, and the religious sympathies of his readers.

In other ways too *The Infidel; or, The Fall of Mexico* shows the shaping power of the literary conventions of Bird's time. First, the very word "fall" in the title places it at once in a body of early nineteenth-century writing that I have elsewhere termed the School of Catastrophe. At the time there was a whole series of poems and plays (and pictures too) on the catastrophic destruction of cities or continents or of the whole world itself. Bryant's poem "The Prairies," Poe's story "The Conversation of Eros and Charmion," Thomas Cole's painting "Destruction," and Bulwer's novel *The Last Days of Pompeii* are well-known examples[6]. To this group Bird's account of the devastation of Tenochtitlan clearly belongs. Second, in *The Infidel*, even more strongly than in *Calavar*, appears the Gothic tradition. All the unnecessary paraphernalia of the nun who has broken her vows, the murderous monk who mysteriously wishes to murder the hero, the secret cross which the hero gives to his beloved, and the deep plots and dark disguises of the villains are directly out of the Gothic novel. The clearest Gothic aspect of the book, however, is the theme of incest. Infeliz, who passionately loves Juan, is his twin sister; only by the beneficent wickedness of the villain and the nobly stupid stubbornness of Juan himself are they prevented from committing the horrible sin. And their disguised father almost kills both of them. Third, the scene near the end of the novel in which Guzman is made to fight Indian warriors in a gladitorial contest is borrowed from a literary tradition of the long series of poems and novels about Rome and Pompeii: nearly every one of these (compare again *The Last Days of Pompeii*) comes to a climax in the arena. Bird, who had made such a success with his own gladiatorial scene in his Roman play, cleverly transfers the conventional incident to Mexico. He even specifically remarks that the Mexicans had "the spirit of the Roman amphitheater." The only wonder is that he has the villain Guzman rather than the hero Juan fight for his life while tied to the great rock.

A fourth literary tradition greatly affects the characterization. In *The Infidel* we find an early example of the conventional distinction in American fiction between the dark, sinful, passionate woman and the fair, weak, and good heroine. Bird has to work rather hard to turn his Indian heroine Zelahualla (in an early version of the story she is blessed with euphonious name Citlaltihuatl) into a blonde, but he manages to describe her as much lighter than the other Indian maidens and indeed as lighter than many of the Spaniards. She is a good girl; she submits gracefully when, in first meeting with her in the book, her lover Juan passionately tries to convert her. Though Juan's whole courtship seems to be a longwinded theological discussion that would be boring from a priest and is ridiculous from a lover, she does not object, even though, if she has a brain in her head, she must see that it is the Christians who are murdering her people and destroying her home. Infeliz, on the other hand, is the supposedly "fallen" woman. According to the nineteenth-century tradition in fiction that a "fallen" woman, even had she not lost her virtue but only her reputation, can never rise again, Infeliz vainly attempts to convince Juan that she is still pure. With the author's apparent approval, he again and again repulses her. Despite all his noble virtue, he will not even consent to hear her explanation of the circumstances that have caused him to believe her impure. When she has saved his life, he rebukes her because it is "unseemly" for a woman to carry a dagger even to defend her own chastity. And when in words she vigorously defends her honor, Juan is "shocked by a fire so unwomanly." Yet we are evidently supposed to admire Juan! Proof that Bird's assessment of his contemporary readers' prejudices was probably correct is provided by a review of *Calavar* which criticizes that novel on grounds of taste and morals because it indelicately allows a woman to appear in boy's clothing.

If anyone in Bird's time could have been a sound critic of *The Infidel*, it would have been William Gilmore Simms, who at the time was a coming writer of romance much like Bird's. Four years later Simms was to publish *The Damsel of Darien* and, fourteen years after that *Vasconselos*, both novels about early days in Spanish America. Writing to Bird's and his mutual friend James Lawson in May, 1835, Simms made a number of apt comments on Bird's novel. He found it too loftily written. All the cavaliers speak the same language. Though he praised Bird for his research and industry, he felt that many of the historical details about Mexican life and superstitions were monotonous and out of place in a romance, which should move quickly. The scenes of gorgeous description were picturesque; but, no matter how skillfully done, too much pageantry became tedious. He particularly criticized Bird's lack of concentration in the novel: there were too many characters and too much mystery; it would have been better with a simpler plot told more clearly and boldly. Similarly, concentration on a few carefully elaborated scenes of Mexican life would have been more effective than Bird's attempt to picture everything.

Simms, it seems to me, is right. Though the stirring scenes of the siege are well executed and the visit of Guatimozin in disguise to Cortez' camp is excellent romantic adventure, there is too much crammed into the novel. Bird's meticulousness with historical detail, however interesting the detail, does frequently interfere with his story. The method of narration is slow. Though in the tradition of Scott, the beginning, a recapitulation of the events since the Battle of Otumba, is awkward and wearisome. And the novel is certainly diffuse.

What Simms says of the characters is also true. There are too many. As a result, most are wooden and conventional. There is a certain spirit in Infeliz which elicits sympathy; Villafana is a very devilish villain; and the Ottomie warrior is attractive. But Cortez and Guzman and Camarga are, on the whole, lifeless. Guatimozin is attractive at first, but Bird so clearly changes his mind about him that he loses his force. By far the most attractive character is Befo, the great and loyal dog. In all the desolation of the fall of Mexico nothing is so sad as the death of Befo! Had only Juan Lerma died (as the romantic hero he lives happily ever after) instead of his better and more intelligent canine friend, the reader would be better satisfied. Befo has force and strength and brains, while, like too many of Bird's heroes, Juan spends most of his time languishing in the last stages of mental or physical exhaustion. Simms calls him a milksop who does nothing, whose only virtue is passive endurance. Certainly he is utterly lethargic. Unfairly charged by Cortez with various crimes and condemned to death, he tamely submits; on the eve of his execution he resists being rescued; he is incredibly magnanimous in forgiving his enemies. He shows no spirit whatsoever.

Supposedly Juan is noble and honorable when he refuses to oppose Cortez and says that he will die on the gallows rather than turn "renegade and apostate." But the reader, instead of thinking him noble, finds him nerveless and foolish. His lofty sentiments sound artificial; they are true only to romances, not to human nature. The reader cordially agrees, I fear, when one of Bird's own characters criticizes him for his "stupid womanish resignation" and another characterizes him as a "sick lambkin." Since we cannot respect Juan, the whole novel—despite its vivid scenes of battle, its exotic pictures of ancient Mexico, the suspense of its exciting incidents, and the historical interest of its narrative—loses much of its power. It is unfortunate that Bird so often weakened his novels by placing at their centers spineless, sickishly noble, and sadly stupid heroes.

CHAPTER 7

Novels of Outlaws and Indians

THOUGH in his first two historical romances Bird had strayed as far afield as Mexico, never again in a completed novel did he set his story outside his own country. Despite novels with foreign settings by Cooper, Simms, and others, the main tendency of American fiction during Bird's time was toward novels on native subjects. American critics at the time, particularly the Young America group centered in Cornelius Mathews and the Duyckincks in New York, were apt to be super-patriotic; readers, too, generally preferred stories laid in America. Furthermore, Bird himself as an author was very open to the inspiration of place: he liked to set his stories in localities which he had actually visited. Thus *The Hawks of Hawk Hollow* is set in his beloved Delaware Water Gap; *Nick of the Woods* was inspired partly by his frequent trips to Kentucky; he was encouraged to proceed with the never-finished novel of American Revolution, *The Volunteers,* by a visit to the site of the Battle of Brandywine; and both Niagara Falls and Mammoth Cave inspired shorter fictional treatments. It is natural, then, that Bird's historical fiction should in large part deal with Delaware, Pennsylvania, and Kentucky.

Throughout his life Bird was interested in the forest and frontier. Whenever he could, he traveled through the backwoods portions of the country—Georgia, Tennessee, Kentucky, parts of Ohio, and the western portions of Pennsylvania. From his friends Doctor Black and John Grimes and others he eagerly sought the legends of the frontier. His book of sketches, *Peter Pilgrim,* includes a story of a night at a backwoods tavern, the bloody tale of an attack by Indians and renegade white men on an Ohio flatboat, and a story of river steamboats that looks forward to

Mark Twain. Indeed, Bird planned a long series of novels about the West, many of them on Indian subjects. In the already mentioned series of "Legends of the New World," the first group was to consist of *The Moccasin Girl, The Sagamore,* and *La Belle Rivière.* A later scheme, for a series to be entitled "Tales of the Fallow Field," was to include *The Carabine, The Clover Patch, Men of the Hills* (an early name for *The Hawks*), *Ipisco Poe* (later published as *A Belated Revenge*), *The Kidnappers,* and *Nick of the Woods.* A further list is entitled "Tales of Kentucky": *The Forest Rover* (on Daniel Boone), *The Blue Licks* (on the battle against the British and Indians fought by frontiersmen there), *The Cohee* (on the famous frontiersman Simon Kenton), and *The Fighting Quaker* (another title for *Nick*). Still another scheme for a group of novels to be called "Tales of the Salt River" included *Nick,* several of the other Kentucky tales, and some of the specifically Indian novels. Bird also planned a novel on the Moravian missionary settlement destroyed by the Indians at Gnadenhutten, Ohio. Fragments of a number of these projected works exist; and although Bird gave up writing novels before he had fully carried out any of these schemes, these fragments and the backwoods novels that he did write place him squarely in the tradition of the frontier novel established by James Hall, Timothy Flint, Cooper, Simms, and J. K. Paulding.

I *The Hawks of Hawk Hollow*

The Hawks of Hawk Hollow, A Tradition of Pennsylvania (1835) was not published until after *Calavar* (1834) and *The Infidel* (1835), but it had been begun much earlier. As Bird himself says in the introduction, much of the inspiration for the novel came from the beauty of the Delaware Water Gap. Bird and his artist friend Grimes had visited the Gap on a camping and sketching trip in 1826 and again in 1827. There they had met a young artist named Birch, perhaps a prototype of the artist Hunter. By 1828, a story called "Men of the Hills" had already been substantially planned, but whether as a tragedy or a romance it is difficult to ascertain. In 1830 Bird definitely planned to write it as a romance, and by 1832 he had even drawn up a still extant draft title page. At various times he seems to have contemplated calling it *Vervallen, The Desert Rover,* and *The Refugee.*

The highly complex plot of *The Hawks* has to do with the Gilbert family who, having been dispossessed of their estates during the Revolution because of their Tory sympathies, have become outlaws and marauders. By devious dealing their lands and mansion have been taken over by a Colonel Falconer, who has also been responsible in some way for the death of a Gilbert girl, Jessie. When the novel opens in 1782, only one of the fierce Gilbert brothers is left alive; but crafty, strong, and brutal Oran Gilbert is a whole band in himself. The romantic hero of the story, whose home is ostensibly in Jamaica, has come to the lovely Delaware Gap country to sketch and paint. Through no fault of his own he is accused of being involved in the murder of Colonel Falconer and the killing of Falconer's young son Harry, and the accusation gains weight when it is discovered that his real name is Hyland Gilbert. Repeatedly Oran Gilbert helps him escape from danger into the forest, but each time, through stupidity or a too fine sense of honor, Hyland allows himself to be recaptured. Finally he is condemned to death. At the last moment he is, of course, saved. It turns out that he is not the full brother of Oran but only a half-brother, his mother having been the Jessie Gilbert whom Falconer seduced. It further evolves that Falconer had secretly married Jessie; therefore Hyland is the legitimate heir to the estate, whereas the proud Harriet Falconer, his half-sister who has been instrumental in Hyland's apprehension on the charge of having murdered Harry Falconer, is illegitimate. Her pride broken, she dies; and, with all the Falconers and Oran Gilbert dead, Hyland can claim the estate as his and happily marry the girl he loves.

Though the Delaware Water Gap provided much of the inspiration for the novel, Bird was certainly stimulated to it by other influences too. One of these is almost surely the legend of the Harp or Harpe brothers of Kentucky, embodied in James Hall's novel *Harpe's Head, or Kentucky. A Tale* (1833), but certainly likely to have been known before that date to anyone as interested in backwoods legend as Bird was. When Hall's book did appear, Grimes immediately wrote to Bird to suggest that here was good material for romance. He said he had not read the book but had "just had a detail of all the particulars of the story of the

Harps and their lawless associates, and it appears to me to be the ground work for something that might be made very good. There are other things and many of them too in the history of the early times of old Kentuck that I think would appear well if well told."[1]

The Harpes—the name evidently suggested the title "Hawks"—were around 1799 the fiercest and most feared outlaws in Kentucky and Tennessee. Like the Hawks of Bird's novel, they spread terror wherever they appeared. One story was that they had originally been Tories and, remaining loyal to the king, continued their depredations on the Americans after the Revolution. The two brothers with their followers appeared mysteriously here and there, often in disguise. Once at least they disguised themselves (like the Hawks' confederate in the novel) as Methodist preachers, and once as peddlers. Caught at last, they broke jail. They were pursued again and again in the wilderness into which they fled on splendid horses. They communicated with each other by means of whistles. They were armed with tomahawks. Finally, stripped of all his followers, Big Harpe was tracked down and killed in much the same way as Oran Gilbert is tracked down (Oran, in contrast, escapes to die by himself). Though Bird makes Oran Gilbert more gallant than Big Harpe and though he saves the story of Harpe joining the Indians for attacks on the settlers for *A Belated Revenge*, it is obvious how much he borrows from the Harpe brothers' careers.

But Bird is, of course, right when he says in his introduction that the tale is not peculiarly American. Irving in "The Legend of Sleepy Hollow" had pointed to the possibilities for adventurous fiction inherent in the exploits of the Tory and the patriot "Cowboys" in the neutral ground near New York, and Cooper had written his novel *The Spy* about just such exploits. Yet the essential situation is as old as the tales of Robin Hood fighting in the forest for his true king. Scott, for example had handled it in *Ivanhoe*. Nor does Bird neglect to fill out the basic story with other material. Into the story of the Tory brothers bitterly fighting in the woods around their family mansion now sequestered into other hands, he introduces one of his usual intricate plots. Colonel Falconer, the villain who seduced his benefactor's daughter and now owns the estate; his dark, spirited daughter, who of course must come to a sad end; the sweet, loving, timid heroine; the gentlemanly real heir, who thinks himself the brother of the outlaws but who is really their nephew; and the "humour" characters like the doctor and the old soldier—these are the ordinary appurtenances of a fictional plot of the age. The actor with his many disguises reminds one of Cooper's Harvey Birch. And in the painter Hunter (later identified as Hyland Gilbert) Bird has incorporated many of the experiences of his friend John Grimes, the itinerant painter. The skill of Hunter in painting a picture of the heroine's dead brother, for instance, reflects the letters to Bird in which Grimes reported that he had gained a reputation for painting pictures of the dead. "I am as regularly called in to paint from dead folks," Grimes wrote, "as the coffin maker is to build them their last house."[2]

With these fundamentally good materials (aside from the fictional plot) Bird achieves some excellent scenes. The near-drowning of Hunter, the breaking up of the wedding, the battles in the forest, and particularly the final chase and escape of Oran Gilbert are exciting. He manages to create considerable suspense, especially in the wedding incident and in Oran's attempts to rescue Hyland from the prison. Yet Bird tries to use too much material, and as a result his good pieces are lost in a welter of plots and counterplots. His characters are far too many. The humorous scenes are almost a dead loss; they remind us strikingly of Bird's early comedies, from which some of them may well have been borrowed. Though in the novel Bird has fortunately changed from the involuted style of the Mexican romances to a clear and direct style, there is still far too much verbiage: much of the book moves slowly. As Poe said in his able review, Bird is always better in scenes of hurry, tumult, and excitement than in the calmer, more philosophical scenes. His forte is the drama of action; his dialogue is a failure.

As usual, the fictional plot is weaker than the semihistorical parts of the book. Concealed marriages, changeling heroes, repentant villains, and blustering soldiers largely get in the way of the story. They seem threadbare, and the unravelling of the complicated situations into which Bird has drawn them is undramatic and dull. Even the scene in which Hyland stands trial for murder, is convicted, and then is cleared is trite. Though he may have appealed to the readers of Bird's time, the hero Hyland Gilbert is utterly impossible for the modern reader to stomach. Much of his time is spent in swooning and despair. When his brother brings him the girl he loves and who loves him, his nice sense of honor forces him to take her back home to marry his rival. When his rival forces him to fight and wounds him, instead of returning the fire he throws his gun away and refuses to defend himself from the other's brutal assault. When his rival is about to be clubbed—deservedly —Hyland interferes to save him. His lack of spirit causes constant deadly danger to his intrepid outlaw brother. If Hyland is the ideal nineteenth-century gentleman, we are well rid of nineteenth-century gentility!

So too when the other characters are going through their conventional novelistic paces, they have little interest. It is only when they break away from fictional conventions that they gain a little life. For instance, near the beginning of the novel we breathe a sigh of relief when the heroine breaks from the tradition of fragility and helplessness and with prompt and courageous action rescues Hunter from the rushing stream into which he has fallen. We cheer because we think Bird is breaking the code of the shrinking violet. But, alas, after this one feat Catherine spends most of her time moping and crying, and, in order to please her old father, she bravely faces marriage with a man she dislikes. When she is kidnapped by her lover and his brother, all she can do is cry piteously to go home. On the other hand, Harriet Falconer, the dark, active girl, starts well as an amateur detective seeking the outlaws. She nearly succeeds. We admire her spirit and practical capability. But, as it must be in nineteenth-century American novels, her unlady-like behavior (objected to, by the way, in a contemporary review in the *Athenaeum*[3]) can lead only to misery. Her beloved brother is killed, her father dies, and she is proved to be illegitimate. Faced with such calamities, her original spirit mysteriously evaporated, all she can do is droop and die. The dark heroine again bites the dust!

Much more interesting are the characters like Oran and the actor Sterling who do not have to conform to the niceties of novelistic convention or who, perhaps more accurately, can be treated (as Scott treats his Rob Roy, and Cooper his Pathfinder and Harvey Birch) as below and thus outside of genteel fictional society. Indeed, Oran is so effective and attractive that we feel Bird has again confused the sympathies of his readers. Oran Gilbert is *said* to be a fierce, lawless, bloodthirsty, unrelenting outlaw harrying the countryside in almost unmotivated savagery, robbing and maiming and killing. He and his band are *said* to be universally detested and feared. But the novel itself presents him far more sympathetically. He seems a bold Robin Hood, who, robbed of his inheritance by evil men, courageously maintains himself in the forest. In Bird's time perhaps the remembrance of the vicious and bloodthirsty Harpes carried over into the novel, casting an evil shadow on Oran and his band; perhaps the cause of the Tories seemed more detestable then than it does today. But certainly to the modern reader Oran's courage, his ingenuity, and above all his loyalty to the brother who attempts to foil many of his schemes seem admirable. We wish, indeed, that Bird had made Oran his hero or at least paid so little attention to his ostensible hero (as Cooper and Scott often do) that we could ignore the upper-class characters in an exciting tale of outlaws. As it is, our sympathies are too much divided, and we are forced to wonder whether Bird himself wholly had thought his story through. *The Hawks of Hawk Hollow,* though a potentially good novel, is not strongly organized or firmly written.

II   *Nick of the Woods*

The next novel of the backwoods was *Nick of the Woods; or, The Jibbenainosay,* Bird's most popular book, which appeared in 1837. A second, revised edition was called for in 1853, and the more than thirty editions published since include translations into German, Polish, and Dutch. Though Bird himself declined to dramatize it, it was turned by several authors into one of the most popular melodramas of the time. G. W. Harby of New Orleans composed a version that was widely played by the tragedian Edmund S. Conner. Even more popular was the version by Louisa H. Medina that was written in 1838 and held the stage for at least twenty years. A third was by a western author named Morden; a fourth was published in England by J. T. Haines.

Nick of the Woods is a story of the Kentucky backwoods. Though there is also a conventional romantic plot, the real story is that of the Quaker Nathan Slaughter, who is thought to be an

inoffensive and indeed timorous hunter unwilling to help the
bolder Kentuckians battle the Indians but who in secret is
really the fiercest Indian fighter of them all. Alone except for
his little dog Peter, he tracks down prowling red men and
slays them in revenge for the massacre by Indians before the
story opens of his wife, children, and mother. On each red
corpse he makes his mark, a bloody cross. To the settlers he is
a mystery; to the Indians he seems a demon, the Jibbenainosay—
or, in English, the Devil or Nick of the Woods.

The story opens as Roland Forrester and his beautiful cousin
Edith, on their way to make a new life for themselves in the
wilderness after the death of their guardian Major Forrester,
enter Bruce's station in frontier Kentucky. The cousins are
forced into the wilderness because a villainous lawyer named
Braxley has produced a will of Major Forrester that leaves all
his estates to an illegitimate daughter long thought dead but
asserted by Braxley to be still living and producible. At Bruce's
station they meet Colonel Bruce and his family, which includes
Telie Doe, daughter of Abel Doe, a renegade white man now
with the Indians, and they watch the mild-mannered Quaker
trapper Nathan Slaughter easily throw Roaring Ralph Stackpole,
the boastful "ring-tailed squealer."

On the following day they set out on their journey but are
delayed because Stackpole has stolen Roland's horse; on account
of the delay they are given no escort. Just as they become
lost in the forest, Telie Doe, who has shown extraordinary
interest in Edith, comes to guide them, and though she urges
them to go to the lower ford, Roland insists on heading for the
upper, despite a mysterious warning he had been given in
the night. They rescue Stackpole from imminent death, meet
Nathan near a slaughtered Indian, and are warned by a fleeing
peddler named Pardon Dodge that enemy Indians are near.
Taking refuge in a deserted cabin, they beat off prolonged
Indian attacks and are finally able to cross the flooded river
but are later captured by Indians paid by the villainous Braxley
through his intermediary Abel Doe. Nathan frees Roland, and
together (with the help of Stackpole, whom they again rescue)
they go to Wenonga's Indian village to try to rescue Edith.
Just as Nathan has almost freed Edith from the hateful Braxley
and the fierce Wenonga, Roland's impatience and Stackpole's

penchant for stealing horses arouse the Indians and cause the capture of all. But as the fire begins to rise about the white men bound to the stake, the valorous Kentucky cavalry rides in to the rescue.

All are saved, Edith by Pardon Dodge as Braxley tries to ride off with her. Telie is revealed as Major Forrester's illegitimate daughter who has been brought up by Doe as his own child at the behest of Braxley. Roland, offered her hand and all the wealth that seemingly goes with it, refuses because of his love for Edith. But Roland is rewarded by the discovery of a later will of Major Forrester, long concealed by Braxley, leaving the money to himself and Edith. Nathan, having slain Wenonga and recovered the scalps of his own murdered wife and children, disappears into the forest, finally convinced that action rather than Quaker peacefulness is what is needed on the frontier.

Bird had been interested in Indian stories from his earliest years. In fact, what is perhaps the earliest extant piece of his fiction is a school composition entitled "The Whitewashed Cottage of the Susquehannah, An Indian Story," which tells in childish style of a fierce Indian attack on a settlement and the capture and escape of the settlers. He had planned a play on King Philip and had completed one on Oralloossa. On his trips to the West he had made special visits to the sites of Indian battles, and many of the early novels he planned were to have been on Indian subjects. He also had been deeply interested for a long time in the dark and bloody ground of Kentucky. Not only had he traveled thither three times, but with characteristic thoroughness he had read widely in books on the West. Indeed, Cecil B. Williams in the scholarly introduction to his excellent edition of *Nick of the Woods* (1939) calls Bird, with perhaps slight exaggeration, "one of the most assiduous of students of Western historical and literary writing of the period." He was surely well prepared to write his novel.

Some time around 1827 Bird heard from his Kentucky friends Black and Grimes the legend of the fighting Quaker that he was to mould into the story of Bloody Nathan. At one time he may have thought of writing a play on the subject, for there is a projected drama listed in his notes under the title *Telie*, the name later used for one of the principal characters of the novel. At another time, when he was projecting a magazine to be called *The Adelphi,* he planned to include in the first issue a twenty-five page story on the subject. As Williams' introduction shows with great detail and perspicuity, Bird worked on the novel for a number of years and, as he proceeded, changed plots and names numerous times. For his book, as Williams also points out, he made a meticulous study of the geography and history of the region in which it was to be set. Most of the places mentioned in the novel can be definitely identified.

In publishing in 1837 a novel on Indians and frontiersmen, Bird was entering an already well-occupied field. Indian stories dated back to the seventeenth- and early eighteenth-century accounts of Indian captivity by such authors as Mary Rowlandson and John Williams. This material was used in fiction as early as Ann Eliza Bleecker's epistolary novel *The History of Maria Kittle,* published in 1797 but written at least fourteen years earlier. The first real use of Indian material in the novel, however, was by Charles Brockden Brown, Bird's predecessor as foremost Philadelphia novelist. Especially in *Edgar Huntley* (1799) Brown had given a vivid picture of his hero battling against savage, sanguinary Indians. The tradition of the Indian novel had been continued by Lydia Maria Child in *Hobomok, A Tale of Early Times* (1824); by J. K. Paulding in *Koningsmarke, the Long Finne* (1823); and, of course, by the first three novels of Cooper's Leatherstocking Tales: *The Pioneers* (1823), *The Last of the Mohicans* (1826), and *The Prairie* (1827). Just two years before the publication of Bird's novel, William Gilmore Simms had sent Bird a copy of *The Yemassee* (1835), the first of his Indian border romances. Nor in considering the tradition of Indian fiction should one forget narrative poems such as the tremendously popular poem *Yamoyden* (1820) by J. W. Eastburn and R. C. Sands, and the several verse legends about Indians by Whittier. Washington Irving's sketches of "Philip of Pokanoket" and other Indian subjects had also contributed to the popularity of the theme.

Though the basic idea of Bird's *Nick of the Woods* undoubtedly came from frontier legend—whether, as seems likely, from a Kentucky legend told him by Black or, as Bird himself asserts in his preface, from a Pennsylvania legend—Bird probably also owes much to other sources.[4] He had read McClung's *Sketches*

of Western Adventure (Williams holds this to have been a
major source), Marshall's *History of Kentucky,* Timothy Flint's
works, and many other books of Western travel and adventure.
He had looked up the history of George Rogers Clark's campaigns
against the Indians in Kentucky, and, perhaps most important
of all, he knew the works of the frontier author Judge James
Hall. Though at the time the figure of the Indian-hater was
a frequent one in Western lore—one finds it in J. K. Paulding's
The Dutchman's Fireside (1831) and even in Melville's *The
Confidence Man* (1857)—Bird almost certainly owes something
directly or indirectly to Hall's story "The Indian Hater" first
published in an annual in 1829. In Hall's story Monson, the
Indian hater, has seen his wife and children and mother and
even his dog burnt to death by Indians in his frontier cabin.
Left alone in the world, his only thought is vengeance. Secretly
and mysteriously he tracks down Indians and kills them with
an insane hatred. The narrator of the story talks to him near
the remains of his clearing and cabin—a site that reminds us
immediately of the ruined cabin in *Nick.*

In Hall's book *Harpe's Head,* which Grimes had mentioned
to Bird in 1833, there is also a hint that Bird might have adopted
for Nathan. Colonel Hendrickson has been a soldier, but he
had become a firm Christian, staunchly resolved to stop fighting,
forgive his enemies, and be a man of peace. But when the
battle with the Indians takes place, his eyes light up with
inhuman ferocity and he thirsts for blood as he seeks vengeance
on the savages for their past butchering of his son. Though he
thought and prayed to overcome it, his hatred welled up, making
him more fierce than any other Indian-fighter. After the battle,
like Quaker Nathan, he is deeply contrite, however, and asks
God's pardon for the blood he has shed. In the same book a
dog serves the Harpes as a watchman just as little dog Peter
serves Nathan. Williams has shown the probable sources of
other elements of the novel in other works on the West by authors
probably known to Bird.

Though it is primarily a novel of adventurous action, Bird
has at least two serious purposes in *Nick of the Woods.* One is
psychological. A doctor of medicine and always interested in
theoretical psychology, he studies with care Bloody Nathan's
dual and contradictory nature. In the mild and pious Quaker

there is a demon of vengeance that bursts forth whenever Nathan has a chance to kill an Indian. Then his whole nature is so changed that he becomes the Devil of the woods. Yet there is no indication that Nathan is not entirely sincere in his pious protestations of peacefulness and in his remorse after his deeds of evil. It is interesting that, as physiologist, Bird indicates that after his bloody deeds Nathan has some kind of epileptic seizures. We only regret that instead of carrying his analysis to a conclusion Bird finally lets Nathan lose his distinctive duality and to some extent at least become an ordinary frontiersman.

The other serious purpose is to paint an accurate, realistic picture of life in frontier Kentucky. Bird in his original preface apologizes for making Colonel Bruce, the captain of the station, so rough; but he defends himself on the grounds of truth to reality. In Ralph Stackpole, the boasting frontiersman, he attempted to catch accurately the dialect of the region and the character of the riproaring frontiersmen of the time. As early as his trip to the South with Forrest in 1833 Bird had meticulously listened for and recorded in his diary the cant words and picturesque speech of the back country, though he had not in reality much cared for the characters who spouted these words. He had written from Tennessee: "I think Hoogers, Roarers, and, in general, all the geniuses of the river and prairie are mighty dull stupid rascals; and I wish I was back in Philadelphia."[5] But in his novel he makes good use of his knowledge of such figures. Of course, as Bird says in his Preface of 1837, the "roarer" is perhaps more legendary than realistic. He is in the tradition of Davy Crockett and has the humorous wild extravagance of language of a Simon Kenton, Pete Featherton, or Mike Fink; and he even owes a little to a passage from Bartram's *Travels*.[6] Though Bird is essentially a highly romantic author, in Stackpole he led the way toward the "Western" humorous characterization that had already been exploited to some extent by Longstreet in his *Georgia Scenes* and that was later to be seized upon by the Western realists like Mark Twain. If Roaring Ralph Stackpole is not, as Rufus Griswold asserted, the original in fiction of the lawless, half-horse, half-alligator species of the Mississippi riverman known as "the ring-tailed roarer from Salt River,"[7] he is certainly close to the source. Though *Nick* is largely a novel of terror, tragedy, and vengeance, in his wish for accuracy Bird also included in it the comic tone of the backwoods.

But the most striking aspect of realism in the book is the treatment of the Indians. Early in his career, as *Oralloossa* and "The Colapeesa" show, Bird had tended to idealize the Indian. During his trip to the South he had gone to see the Creeks, hoping to verify his "old visions of romance." He had seen "the proud warriors" in the Muscogee groves—but, alas, "they always came to sell green strawberries, and beg tobacco."[8] Among the Creeks he had seen one noble, proud, and lofty brave, fierce and Apollo-like (the usual comparison of the time), but that one seems to have been unique. Bird did feel keenly the injustice of the settlers' taking land from the Indians. But by the time he wrote *Nick of the Woods* Bird, perhaps from his travels through the frontier, had assimilated the feelings of the frontiersman toward the savages. Thus in the novel they are "red niggurs," dirty and drunken, with an unquenchable blood-lust. The frontiersmen, who are nearly as savage (they, too, delight in taking scalps), slaughter them like rattlesnakes. Though Bird does not express approval of the extremes to which the whites go, he certainly makes the reader sympathize with Nathan's wish for bloody vengeance, and he pictures the Indians as a brutish race who must inevitably be destroyed by the advance of white civilization. He will stand for no romanticizing or sentimentalizing of the Indians. He pictures them laughing at the sufferings of their captives, he shows them striking the dead bodies of their foes in a mad fury of mutilation, and he comments in Chapter XX:

Such is the red-man of America, whom courage,—an attribute of all lovers of blood, whether man or animal; misfortune,—the destiny, in every part of the globe, of every barbarous race, which contact with a civilized one cannot civilize; and the dreams of poets and sentimentalists have invested with a character wholly incompatible with his condition. Individual virtues may be, and indeed frequently are, found among men in a natural state; but honor, justice, and generosity, as characteristics of the mass, are refinements belonging only to an advanced state of civilization.

In Chapter XXXIV he remarks that though "the familiar of a Spanish Inquisition has sometimes moistened the lips of a heretic stretched upon the rack,—and the Buccaneer of the tropics has relented over the contumacious prisoner gasping to death under his lashes and heated pincers," the fiendish Indian, once he has begun to torture a victim at the stake, has never been known "to regard with any feelings but those of exultation and joy, the agonies of the thrice wretched victim." And even in the preface to the first edition, before he had been criticized for his treatment of the Indians, Bird said, "The North American savage has never appeared to me the gallant and heroic personage he appears to others." The American Indian is, Bird claims, the only race in the world that wantonly wars not only on men but also on women and children.

In picturing the Indian as a bloodthirsty "varmint" Bird was aligning himself with the more realistic authors who wrote about the red man of the frontier. Irving had pictured the Indian as noble and oppressed; the authors of *Yamoyden* had emphasized the greed and cruelty of the white man toward the innocent Indian; and Cooper, though his novels show many villainous Indians, had pictured Uncas and Chingachgook as loyal, courageous, noble heroes of the forest. But other authors had expressed sentiments much closer to the frontiersman's classic assertion that "the only good Indian is a dead Indian." The actual frontiermen's accounts of their struggles were almost all on Bird's side of the question, and many of the literary writers too had emphasized the cruel and treacherous side of the Indian. Paulding in *Koningsmarke*, indeed, had tried to take a middle ground: he showed Indian atrocities but also pointed out the reasons for them. But Charles Brockden Brown had portrayed the red men as merciless and murderous, James Hall had pictured them massacring women and children, and Bird's contemporary Simms, in *The Yemassee*, had emphasized the frontiermen's burning hatred of them. Bird placed himself firmly in this anti-idealizing, anti-romantic camp.

As a result Bird found himself sharply attacked by those who thought that he had been too harsh in his pictures of both frontiersmen and Indians. He was even accused, because of his picture of Bloody Nathan, of being prejudiced against Quakers. The criticism of his portrayal of Indians, however, was the strongest. It was summed up in the preface that the British novelist Harrison Ainsworth wrote for an English edition of *Nick of the Woods*. Ainsworth, with national animosity, accused Bird of painting the Indians as black as possible in order to justify the vicious persecutions and robbery of lands they suffered at the hands of American pioneers. He felt Bird's novel was in part American self-justificatory propaganda directed at Europe. Bird was angered by Ainsworth's criticism. When in 1852-53 he revised *Nick* for the edition published by J. S. Redfield, he added a new preface in which he defended himself. He argued that he had no worse desire "than to make his delineations . . . as correct and true to nature as he could." He had sought, he said, "to construct such a story, marked by such events and characters, as would illustrate the more remarkable features of frontier life in the not yet forgotten days of frontier heroism."

> The savage and the man who fought and subdued the savage— the bold spirits who met him with his own weapons in his own hunting-grounds and villages, and, with a natural vengeance, retaliated in the shadow of his own wigwam some few of the cruel acts of butchery with which he so often stained the hearthstones of the settler—necessarily formed the writer's *dramatis personae;* and if he drew his Indian portraits with Indian ink, rejecting the brighter pigments which might have yielded more brilliant effects, and added an "Indian-hater" to the group, it was because he aimed to give, not the appearance of truth, but truth itself—or what he held to be truth—to the picture.

Bird goes on to ridicule the idealized Indians of Chateaubriand, Marmontel, and Cooper (he could have added his own Oralloossa) as poetical illusions and popular stereotypes without foundation in fact. Such characters as Atala and Uncas, nature's noblemen, the chevaliers of the forest, are "beautiful unrealities and fictions merely." In reality, though the Indian may be a gentleman, "he is a gentleman who wears a very dirty shirt, and lives a very miserable life, having nothing to employ him or keep him alive, except the pleasures of the chase and the scalp-hunt—which we dignify with the name of war." It is interesting that the historian Parkman, when describing the anger of the settlers against the

Indians, came stoutly to Bird's defense and cited "the spirited story of Nick of the woods" as the kind of theme which held great promise for American novelists.[9]

The faults of *Nick of the Woods* are those of the novels already discussed. Woven into the excellent frontier background and exciting incidents of battle and capture and escape is a complicated and wholly unbelievable story of concealed wills, villainous kidnapping, changeling babies, and underhanded double-crossing that is finally straightened out only with long explanations and tremendous difficulty. Braxley is merely the conventional villain of stage melodrama, only perhaps a little more stupid in overreaching himself: instead of destroying or hiding away the original will, he carries it around in the wilderness in his pocket whence it can be filched by his confederate Abel Doe and finally recovered by the rightful heirs. The beautiful heroine Edith is pasteboard. The hero, appropriately named Roland in the grand style, is foolish, inconsiderate, full of class consciousness, but superlatively brave. He is a gentleman, with all the tomfoolery which that signifies to Bird. Again and again his stupidity, his unwillingness to listen to reason, and his overfine sense of honor endanger everyone. With perfectly good conscience, because he is a "gentleman," he can be utterly ungrateful to Nathan and Stackpole. When it is proposed that he marry Telie Doe, now an heiress, his "honor and integrity" prevent him, but we have the feeling that these are merely fancy terms for class snobbery. As so often in Cooper, the romantic hero in *Nick of the Woods* is not the real hero at all.

For the life of the book lies in the more realistic, middle- or lower-class characters. Colonel Bruce, the rough but kindly captain of the station, is (as Bird himself averred) an attractive picture of a leading frontiersman. His son Tom is a believable youth longing for the distinction of battle against the Indians. While the upper-class melodramatic villain Braxley is colorless— or overcolored—the coolly calculating renegade Abel Doe (based in part on Simon Girty) arouses real interest because he is not too villainous. His daughter Telie, though far too slightly sketched, is the most humanly appealing person in the novel. Her character, at once retiring and courageous, downtrodden yet loyal, arouses our sympathy greatly. About her and her father we long to know far more than we are told. Of course, as the "other woman" in the book, she is fated to fade away and die in the conventional way, but she is far more interesting and worthy of Roland (if Roland were worth anything) than Edith. Even Pardon Dodge, the cowardly Yankee peddler who gains courage, is well sketched. And Ralph Stackpole, the roaring boaster whose horse-thieving propensities bring on so much disaster, is a living and vital character from Western comic legend.

But the real hero of the novel and the personage who gives it its power is, of course, Nathan Slaughter. Like Cooper's Natty Bumppo he is a lonely wanderer who can never really be comfortable in any settled society. With only his little Peter for company—he has not even the companionship of a Chingachgook —he roams the frontier, derided by the rough pioneers for his Quaker principles and, as the Jibbenainosay, feared by the Indians like the very Devil. With mad vengeance constantly warring in his soul against his sincere belief in non-violence, he can never be truly happy, for the fierce joy of battle can end only in humiliation and contrition of spirit. He can befriend the other characters of the book, but he can never be of them. Like the cowboy hero of a Western or like Natty Bumppo, at the end he can only stride off into the sunset followed by his faithful dog, and Bird's attempt to wind up his novel by domesticating him is a weakness. In him Bird has created or made use of a legendary figure, but more than most such figures Nathan Slaughter has been given an understandable and human psychology. He seems a person as well as a myth. As Vernon Parrington says in his *Main Currents in American Thought,* the Jibbenainosay, the "uncanny figure" of the forest who attacks "with appalling suddenness" the unsuspecting savage, is "one of the most striking and fearful figures of our early fiction."[10] Had the novel, as Williams says, emphasized him even more, it would have been a better book.

Though the romantic plot of villains and wills and changelings is foolishness, the action of the novel is exciting and vivid. Bird keeps firm control over it, and these scenes in frontier Kentucky seem far more immediate and thrilling than even the best of his pageants of action set in Mexico. There is still some of Bird's unfortunate verbiage (at one point he calls a valley an "alluvion"!). Like Cooper's, Bird's characters hold excessively long-winded conversations when they are in the very jaws of danger. Many of the incidents are conventional (or have become so): the travelers are led astray in the woods by a deceptive and incompetent guide; the crafty accomplice overreaches himself in the Indian village; the secreted hero overhears the villains' plotting; at the last moment, when the prisoners are bound to the stake and the torches lighted, the United States calvary comes sweeping down to the rescue. We can understand how *Nick* is a progenitor of the dime novel.

But the tense wanderings through the forest, the fight between young Tom Bruce's party and the Indians, the siege at the ruined Ashburn cabin, and the spying out of the Indian village by Nathan are exciting. The story moves quickly; the scenes, especially those in the Kentucky forests through which Bird himself had traveled, are sharply delineated; and the suspense is built up intensely. Even the dog Peter (we remember Befo in *The Infidel*) adds his bit of comic pathos. Certainly this novel, in regard both to the vitality of the characters and the excitement and intensity of the action, is Bird's best.

III   *A Belated Revenge*

Bird's third novel of the backwoods in *Ipsico Poe, The Long Hunter*, published by Frederick Mayer Bird as *A Belated Revenge* in the November, 1889, issue of *Lippincott's Magazine*. Bird evidently began writing it immediately after the completion of *Nick of the Woods* in the spring of 1837. He planned it as a full two-volume novel, and the tremendous number of extant fragments of it show that, though he never completed this novel, he put a great deal of work into it. Perhaps he found that it was too difficult to dramatize into action the middle sections, which in the published version are given in mere outline summary. This was also one of the periods in his career during which his health was poor. In any case, many years after Bird's death his son finished and edited the novel for *Lippincott's*, of which he was then editor.

A Belated Revenge is a stirring tale of backwoods Virginia in the middle of the eighteenth century. The narrator Ipsico Poe, a young boy when the story opens, finds in the mountains a personable and persuasive young man named Rover who asserts that he is a cousin. Introduced to Ipsico Poe's family, Rover, with his charm and double-dealing, turns all to evil: he kills Ipsico's brother Gregory in ambush; stirs up trouble between Ipsico and his beloved Fanny; persuades Ipsico to leave home and then tries to murder him in a cave; and finally, by marrying Fanny, causes her and her child's deaths. Ipsico, returning after years of captivity with the Indians, tracks Rover (really a renegade, half-Indian cousin named Craven) with the help of the frontiersman Nelson; sees his father killed by Rover; and then, guided by dreams sent by dead Fanny, finds him in a hideaway. After long palaver he kills him there. Some of the characterization and adventures of the renegade Craven, especially the description of his final lurking place, may be based on legends of the Harpes. The incident in the cave owes something to the story, repeated by Bird in his article on Mammoth Cave in *Peter Pilgrim*, that the petrified bodies of men and a dog had been found in a cave in East Tennessee.

Ipsico's guidance by dreams sent from sainted Fanny and his unrealistically great compunctions over killing the scoundrel Craven weaken the story. The tale is also weak in that the whole middle part is not dramatized but merely related to Ipsico, after he has returned home in disguise, by an old man named Matthews. Perhaps, in addition, the reader suspects too soon that the supposed Rover is really Craven. But despite these faults the story is full of strong suspense and vigorous action. The dialect is well handled.

Though Ipsico is another of Bird's too-virtuous suffering heroes, Bird has the skill to work out his history so that every seemingly minor and understandable mistake turns to utter tragedy for him. Yet through Fanny's ghostly help he does finally gain his "belated revenge." Craven, an attractive villain, always has a motive; he is not villainous merely for villainy's own sake. His ability to seem honorable and kindly and his loyalty to his little Indian son are human qualities that many of Bird's villains lack. The characterization of the Regulator, the frontiersman Nelson, is excellent Western local color. It is a fine touch that when Ipsico returns after having tracked down and killed Craven, Nelson chides him for not having brought back his scalp. Ipsico, however, in what may have been a real frontier custom, does bring back tokens of those he has killed to lay on the graves of their victims.

Though we could well dispense with Ipsico's vision of Fanny and Gregory waiting for him in heaven, the novel ends well in its description of Ipsico turning frontiersman, since he has nothing to hold him in Virginia, and in its strong defense of frontier attitudes toward Indians. An Eastern clergyman may argue that murder is evil and wrong, but Ipsico asserts that he cannot repent his killing of Craven: one cannot love and forgive renegade white men and scalping Indians who kill those one loves. This final emphasis on the unsentimental code of the frontier—we wonder whether the passage was written by Bird himself or by Frederick Mayer Bird—is much more convincing than the awkward earlier attempt to absolve Ipsico from the guilt of murder by showing him as a mere instrument of heaven under the guardianship of angelic Fanny.

CHAPTER 8

Satirical Novels of American Character and Society

A THIRD TYPE of novel written by Robert Montgomery Bird is the satirical. From the beginning of his career Bird had now and again turned toward satire. At least two of his early comedies, *The City Looking Glass* in particular, contain considerable mockery of American types and American life. A number of Bird's prose sketches, like "My Friends in the Madhouse" in *Peter Pilgrim,* also have a satirical bent. Later, in his newspaper editorials on political and social affairs, he showed in another way his keen critical interest in the American scene of his era.

At one time Bird projected a whole series of novels "to illustrate American character and society." Among these works he planned but never completed were *Tony, or the Ortocrat,* a novel intended to satirize social classes in America; *Peter Jones, Aeronaut,* a satiric story of a voyage to the moon; and *Tom Binnacle,* evidently a novel of the sea, perhaps the allegorical novel of a voyage to strange Arctic lands, elsewhere called *The North Pole.* Two others were to be called *The "Summum Bonum"* and *Connor, or the Cousins.* In addition (or perhaps this is *The "Summum Bonum"* under another title), he planned to satirize the contemporary feminist movement in *The Letters and Memorials of the Celebrated Mrs. Munchovy: Illustrating the Progress of the New Philosophy.* Several portions of this last work were actually written.

Two books which do "illustrate American character and society" were completed—*Sheppard Lee,* published anonymously in 1836, and *The Adventures of Robin Day,* Bird's last novel, published in 1839. In these two books Bird was following a number of well-established trends in American fiction. In satirizing various aspects of American life through picaresque fiction, for instance, he was in the tradition of Hugh Henry Brackenridge's *Modern Chivalry* (1792-1815) and especially of Royall Tyler's *The Algerine Captive* (1797). Indeed, the similarity of *Robin Day* to the latter is striking. Both are picaresque novels, satirical in their early parts, with adventures in Philadelphia and the South, with stories of slavery and capture by pirates, and with satire on education and medical quackery. *Sheppard Lee* follows the tradition of novels of psychology and pseudo-science introduced into America by Charles Brockden Brown, carried to its height in the works of Poe, and later used by Hawthorne. The name I. Dulwer Dawkins for the fashionable young spendthrift in the same book probably indicates satirical imitation of the Silver Fork School of novels of high society popularized by E. Bulwer-Lytton and Disraeli. Furthermore, Bird's plans for the two allegorical-satirical books, *The North Pole* and *Peter Jones, Aeronaut,* remind one forcibly of Poe's *Narrative of Arthur Gordon Pym of Nantucket* (1838) and of Melville's much later *Mardi* (1849). In the book on the North Pole Bird was planning to satirize American life through the description of a strange civilization found in the extreme Arctic region; Peter Jones was by mistake to sail off in his balloon to the moon, where he too was to find civilizations absurdly similar to those on earth. Both in his plans for these books and in *Sheppard Lee*, Bird is a pioneer in American science fiction.

I *Sheppard Lee*

Sheppard Lee is the story of a man whose soul, by a process of involuntary metempsychosis (how deeply Poe was interested in this subject!), passes from his original body into a dead body and then by acts of will into the dead bodies of five other persons. Sheppard Lee, a young man of moderate wealth, dissipates his fortune in investigating various ways of life but rejecting all of them while the dishonest overseer of his estate cheats him. Reduced to penury, as a last hope he starts digging on his farm for Captain Kidd's treasure. After an accident, he falls into a trance from which he awakens to find himself a disembodied spirit. He finally stumbles upon and enters the body of rich Squire Higginson of Philadelphia.

As Higginson, he is indicted for the murder of Sheppard Lee, whose body has been discovered, but he is released for lack of evidence. Despite his new wealth, Lee finds life as Higginson made intolerable by severe gout and a perverse and shrewish wife. He is therefore glad when he finds he can enter the body of the dandy I. Dulwer Dawkins, who has just committed suicide. But he finds that life as a young man about town supporting himself by "plucking" young rustics is not so pleasant as he might wish. Constantly dodging duns is no fun. Hence, when he finds himself engaged to elope with two well-to-do young ladies on the same night, he is not sorry to creep into the body of Abram Skinner, the old miser and moneylender. Soon tired of Skinner's hateful life, he searches long before he can find another unoccupied body but finally finds that of a philanthropic Quaker who has just been murdered by a convict he was attempting to help. Philanthropy turns out to be no more enjoyable than miserliness: as Zachariah Longstraw, he discovers that those whom he helps are invariably ungrateful and that his principal coadjutor in philanthropy is a hypocritical swindler. Just as Longstraw has learned his lesson and has regained his fortune through the help of his unphilanthropic nephew, he is kidnapped by Yankee peddlers who take him down South to sell him as an Abolitionist.

In order to avoid death by lynching, he becomes a Negro slave, Tom, the pampered servant of a kind and good master. But inflamed by an Abolitionist pamphlet, he joins other rebel slaves in attacking his master's house. For this crime he is hanged, but his buried body is dug up by an anatomist and brought back to life by galvanism. Knowing that he will be hanged again if he is caught, in the excitement Lee enters the body of a bored, lazy young gourmet and idler, Mr. Megrim, who has been frightened to death by the experiment which has revived Tom. Since life as Megrim is merely boredom and dyspepsia and even temporary melancholia, he is glad when he is taken to the scientific show of a German doctor who has developed a new process of mummification by which he has preserved Sheppard Lee's original body. Leaping into his own body, Lee puts the crowd into an uproar by escaping at top speed. He runs 180 miles in three days and finally reaches home safely. He finds that his formerly delapidated farm has been put into good order and made profitable by his brother-in-law and that it is his to take back. Actually he has lain sick for a number of months, during which he has been carefully tended by his sister and the German doctor, and all his experiences after his first accident have been hallucinations. He becomes a steady and contented farmer.

The first chapter of *Sheppard Lee* predicts that the book will be of interest to two classes of readers: the learned and the unlearned. Bird thus hints that he has two main interests in the novel. As a psychologist, metaphysician, doctor of medicine, and physiologist, he took great interest in the relationship between body and spirit. Already in *Nick of the Woods* he had examined the dual personality of Nathan Slaughter. He had studied much about psychological matters and had even given semiscientific lectures on apparitions. In his tale of Sheppard Lee Bird amusingly raises a great many serious psychological and spiritual questions, including that of the influence of the body's physical form and make-up on emotional and intellectual aspects of character. Through the old German doctor he is also able to inject scientific speculation about photography, later to become one of Bird's favorite hobbies. Thus for the learned reader *Sheppard Lee,* far from being wholly fanciful, has a substratum of stimulating thought.

The other and more obvious aim of the novel is, of course, satire on America. For this the plan is excellent. As idle heir of a successful farmer, as rich Squire Higginson, as the penniless dandy I. Dulwer Dawkins, as Abram Skinner the miser and moneylender, as Zachariah Longstraw the cheated Quaker philanthropist, as the Negro slave Tom in the South, and as the wealthy and bored young Mr. Megrim, Sheppard Lee sees almost all aspects of American life, both in the North and in the South. He might well have seen even more; for according to one plan for the novel Bird was to make him, in addition, a physician, a patriot, the President of the United States, a schoolboy, a schoolmaster turned author, and a Yankee peddler adventuring in the West. But through the experiences that Lee does have, Bird directs many a satiric barb at American gambling, agriculture, marriage, business, philanthropy, politics, Abolitionism, law, and dilettantism. A number of the incidents of this essentially picaresque novel—the metempsychosis does not prevent all the adventures from being those of the one ne'er-do-well

Sheppard Lee—are essentially comic. The part in which Lee becomes I. Dulwer Dawkins is really little more than a better retelling in prose narrative of parts of Bird's early comedies *News of the Night* and *The City Looking Glass*. Much of it is farce, just as the shrewish wife of Squire Higginson is a character from comedy or burlesque. Indeed, Bird originally planned the section on the Quaker philanthropist Longstraw as a stage comedy.

But in other parts of the book the satire is deeply serious. It is especially so in the incident in which Longstraw, kidnapped by Yankee peddlers, is carried down South to be sold to Southerners as an Abolitionist, a prime victim for a lynching bee. Bird's satire on the candidate and the mob in Virginia, which turns from oratory about American liberty to the brutal lynching of Longstraw, is bitter. But sharpest of all is the satire in Lee's adventure as the Negro slave Tom. He has a good master; he and his fellow slaves are well treated and content. But an Abolitionist pamphlet is smuggled to them; supposedly it is aimed peaceably at the white masters to urge them to free their slaves, but in reality it is intended as an incendiary tract (particularly in its illustrations) calculated to cause a slave rebellion. The slaves spell out the pamphlet and look at the pictures. From happy and peaceable workers they are changed into demons. They attack the good master's mansion and murder him. They rage through the house like beasts. In order to save her sister from a worse fate, the elder of the master's two young daughters—both of whom had made a special pet of Tom—throws her sister from the cupola of the house to her death on the pavement below and then jumps after her. The author of the antislavery play *The Gladiator*, it should be remembered, was also the man who wished to move out of Pennsylvania if Negroes were given the franchise there!

Though there is too much moralizing in the book, Bird skillfully and successfully uses the opportunities offered by his clever framework. Many of the whimsical scenes are highly amusing. The pictures of real life are vivid. The book is tightly and neatly organized, entertaining as a story, and revealing as a picture of the times. The first-person narrative maintains the continuity, while the various sections provide wide variety. Most of the metamorphoses from one body to another are believably contrived. In each section Bird changes his style so as to conform to the personality with which Sheppard Lee is currently invested. Bird manages some excellent epigrams, and the parody of the Southern campaign speech, though biting, is delightful.

In a shrewd review, however, Poe criticized the basic structure. First, he thought the device of metempsychosis was awkward and unnecessary. Why not create seven different characters to depict the seven aspects of American life rather than requiring the one hero partially to retain and partially to lose his identity through his various transformations? Secondly, Poe thought that if metempsychosis were to be introduced at all, it should be treated seriously. He objected to the conclusion of the novel in which it turns out that all Sheppard Lee's experiences have been hallucinations caused by a blow on the head.[1]

The answer to Poe's first criticism, it seems to me, is that the continuing identity of Sheppard Lee gives the book unity. It also raises psychological and physiological questions in which Bird was interested. In Poe's second criticism he is taking *Sheppard Lee* too ponderously. Bird, though some of his satire (such as his Swiftian scheme for turning dead bodies into manure) is harsh, intends a generally light tone. To take the metempsychosis too seriously is to destroy the tone of clever *jeu d'esprit* that Bird successfully maintains. To do so also distracts attention from the satire which is Bird's main purpose. It is interesting that, despite his criticism, Poe may have drawn ideas from *Sheppard Lee* for two of his short stories. Poe's "The Gold Bug" may owe something to the incident in which Lee digs under a tree in the forest for Captain Kidd's treasure; several details in his story "Some Words with a Mummy" recall the scene in Bird's book in which, after he has been hanged and buried, Sheppard Lee's disinterred body (as the slave Tom) is roused to life by a galvanic electrical shock.[2]

II *The Adventures of Robin Day*

Though Bird's last novel, *The Adventures of Robin Day,* in its published form is much more a novel of lurid picaresque adventure than of satire, it shows signs of having been originally conceived as satirical. The story is the first-person narrative of Robin Day, a castaway orphan picked up by wreckers on a beach near Barnegat, New Jersey. He lives for seven years with a thieving old hag who then sells him to brutal Captain Duck for a keg of rum. After he has saved a little boy from drowning, the boy's father, kindly Doctor Howard, clothes Robin Day, takes him into his own home, and treats him as he does his own son and daughter. Incensed by the tyranny of the brute of a schoolmaster McGoggin, Robin Day takes part in a schoolboy riot in which the schoolmaster is seemingly killed. Furnished with money by Doctor Howard and thinking they will be pursued as murderers, Robin and Doctor Howard's son flee, but on their way to Philadelphia they are robbed. Subsequently Robin is innocently involved in a robbery in Philadelphia; he escapes apprehension only to find himself fighting by mistake with the British in the War of 1812.

Captured by the Americans, he manages to escape again and then sells quack medicines in company with the same thief who had earlier deceived him in Philadelphia. He fights the Indians on the Southern frontier, is captured, and barely escapes dying at the stake. He is taken prisoner by the Spanish in Florida; he turns pirate in the waters near Cuba; he fights his own shipmates in order to save a beautiful young girl, with whom he falls in love; and he and the girl almost die of thirst as they are cast away at sea in a small boat. Into this long series of adventures comes again and again the maleficent figure of Captain Hellcat Brown, first as the highwayman who robbed Robin on the way to Philadelphia and then as thief, Indian-fighter, traitor, and pirate. Robin Day finally turns out to be the son of a rich Spanish American planter who had been murdered by Duck and Brown while on board ship, the ship then having been scuttled. By means of a rosary preserved from his childhood Robin proves his identity but finds out (the same theme had occurred in *The Infidel*) that the girl with whom he has fallen passionately in love is his sister. But in this novel no tragedy results: Robin instantaneously changes his feelings from those of a lover to those of a brother and happily proceeds to marry the daughter of Doctor Howard, his old protector.

The earlier parts of the book are of considerable interest. There Bird seems really anxious to portray, in somewhat satiric terms, a number of aspects of American life. The pictures of the Barnegat wreckers, though only briefly sketched in, have local color. The chapters on the schoolboys and their rebellion against their brutal master McGoggin, based directly on Bird's own experiences at New Castle Academy (Nanna Howard, for instance, is a fictional portrait of Bird's beloved cousin Dorcas), give an amusing and biting picture of an American school of the period. Into the schoolboy revolt Bird interjects parodies of adult campaign oratory and satire on government and politics. He also takes up the then seriously debated question of the advisability of flogging schoolboys. As the novel proceeds, the reader is given a picture of low and high life in Philadelphia, especially of the relationship between the races there; of the methods and success of a quack doctor in Virginia; and of the raising of militia for the Indian wars in Tennessee.

But the latter half of the novel includes a series of wild adventures and coincidences almost too silly and improbable even for a comic strip. Bird lets his fertility in imagining melodramatic situations run wild. Beginning with the adventures in the Indian country, the story becomes utterly incredible, particularly in the constant reappearance under various disguises (reminiscent of Melville's *The Confidence Man*) of the devilish Captain Brown. Though Bird hurries his fantastically complicated plot to an abrupt conclusion, his speed is hardly great enough to please the reader.

Despite its basic weakness *Robin Day* has a number of amusing and telling parts, the dialogue is often pithy and realistic, and the comedy is frequently funny. The scenes in Philadelphia, for instance, do better in fiction what Bird had unsuccessfully tried to do in his early dramatic comedies set in that city. Though technically Robin Day's crimes are not committed intentionally, Bird has at last given up his noble weak hero in favor of a stronger picaresque one. Indeed, bloody Captain Hellcat himself can at one point say admiringly of Robin that he has "a touch of the hellcat in him" too. How often we long for such a "touch" in namby-pamby Juan Lerma, Hyland Gilbert, and Roland Forrester! Perhaps it is a pity that Bird wrote no more novels. If he could have sunk to an utterly despicable hero, he might have written a truly superb novel!

CHAPTER 9

Peter Pilgrim and Other Prose

IN ADDITION to his six novels, Bird wrote a considerable number of shorter prose pieces, some fiction, some non-fiction. In 1838 he collected the best of these into the two volumes of *Peter Pilgrim; or, A Rambler's Recollections*, the title of which echoes S. G. Goodrich's famous pseudonym Peter Parley. But a number of Bird's stories and articles were never collected from the periodicals in which they appeared. Still others remain in manuscript, never having been published at all. And, lastly, Bird planned numerous books and shorter pieces of non-fiction that he never managed to write.

I *Peter Pilgrim*

The introduction to *Peter Pilgrim* shows that it is in part the volume of sketches of travel which Bird planned as early as his Southern and Western trip with Forrest in 1833. Bird says there that he likes to travel to the unvisited portions of his own country—of America. Like Irving, he praises the beauty of New World scenery, but unlike Irving he does not regret the absence of the ruins and castles that tell of man's baseness in the Old World. In the forest and in man himself Bird can find interests that replace those offered by Europe. With pride, then, though with a characteristically American backward glance at Europe, Bird presents his sketches of "scenery and character, life and manners; anecdotes, legends, observations" of his country.

The most interesting parts of the book are the stories of the West. "The Extra Lodger," an amusing story of a Yankee peddler's clever trick to get himself a bed in a crowded and inhospitable inn in the mountains of Virginia, gives a dramatic insight into the discomforts of traveling in backwoods America. "The Arkansas Emigrants" presents an unusual picture of pioneers. In it, the emigrants, an old Virginia family forced West by hard times, are reluctant and regretful settlers of the West. They should have far preferred to stay at home. "The Bloody Broadhorn," an exciting tale supposedly told to the narrator in the 1830's by a man on a steamboat on the Ohio, contrasts by implication the safety and comfort of nineteenth-century river travel with the dangers of flatboating on the Ohio in 1791. The story is of a treacherous and bloody attack on Colonel Storm's flatboat by Indians and a renegade white man. Storm and his beautiful daughter are saved only by a spectral figure in a canoe who, though wounded, manages to kill several Indians and to free the flatboat so that it floats to safety. The "spectral Indian" of the canoe—we remember Mark Twain's story of a ghostly barrel—is really a faithful suitor of Storm's daughter; he had been left behind through the machinations of the villain but had loyally followed the overconfident party in order to save it from disaster. The story paints a vivid picture of old flatboating days on the Ohio.

A fourth story, "A Tale of a Snag" (reprinted from the *American Monthly Magazine*), is also a river story but deals with the Mississippi rather than the Ohio. It concerns an Englishman named Sniggins on a Mississippi steamboat. Having been told tall tales of the deadly snags in the river (Bird once planned a whole volume on steamboat wrecks), Sniggins dreams that the steamboat has hit one in the night and thinks the Americans are "quizzing" him when they assure him that it has not. The interest of the story lies partly in its "Western" humor and in its tales of river life but even more in Bird's own pictures of the monotonous solitude yet boundless power and majestic vitality of the river itself. Comparison with Mark Twain is again inescapable.

Different from these stories of the West are two moral fables, the first closely related to Bird's own poem "The Cave." Though placed in backwoods East Tennessee, based on the popular Kentucky legend of Jonathan Swift and his Blue Jackets, and fitted up with appropriate American scenery and local color, "The Legend of Merry the Miner" harks back through Irving's *Alhambra* and Beckford's *Vathek* to Spanish or Oriental legend.

It is the story of an old Spanish miner who, seeking gold, moves further and further West till one day his dog leads him to a cave where there is gold in great quantities. In the cave are the petrified figure of Pre-Adamite races whose dead forms present an allegory of the evils of the strife for wealth. Merry, too, begins to turn to stone but by prayer escapes, with no gold, to become devout and industrious for a few years. When his lust for wealth returns and he again tries to find the mysterious cave, it has disappeared, but he searches till his lonely death. Throughout the fable Bird is criticizing through moral allegory and sometimes through satire the materialistic values of American society.

His satire is even clearer in "My Friends in the Madhouse," a fable in the eighteenth-century manner closely related to Bird's *Sheppard Lee* and to his interest in abnormal psychology. On a visit to a madhouse a medical student has it proved to him by the patients that not only is he himself mad because he has entered the medical profession but that the whole world outside the institution is mad. The proposals for which each of the patients—the politician, editor, critic, duellist, and truth-teller— have been thought mad are really eminently sane and sensible. It is the world that is mad. Bird's satire is clever and topical. One suggestion, interesting in a story appearing as early as 1838, is that the way to abolish slavery is to substitute machines for manual labor.

In any book of sketches of American Bird would not have been likely to omit mention of two of his favorite places—Niagara Falls and Mammoth Cave. Like his friend Forrest, he was always enthusiastic about the Falls and he visited them whenever he could. He early wrote a poem on Niagara; the full title of the early comedy *News of the Night* includes the name; and, though Sheppard Lee cares for few other sights in his travels, he is greatly impressed and pleased by Niagara. Bird was even more fascinated with Mammoth Cave. In spite of the great difficulties of travel through the backwoods, he repeatedly returned to explore it. He wrote ecstatic letters describing his longing to stay not four but forty days in the cave and telling of his fascination with its thousands of galleries and countless pits. Caves appear repeatedly in his writings too: a cave is the main locale of "The Legend of Merry the Miner"; the hero of *A Belated Revenge* is trapped in a cave· a cave is a refuge for outlaws in *The Hawks of Hawk Hollow;* Mammoth Cave itself is the subject of Bird's longest poem. At one time he projected a work to be called *A Month in the Mammoth Cave,* to be published in a series of five parts and to be illustrated with twenty-five plates. Another plan was for a richly illustrated volume on *Caves and Waterfalls of America.*

It is not suprising, then that *Peter Pilgrim* includes "A Night on the Terrapin Rocks," a Poe-like account of a terrifying night spent on the slippery verge of the great falls. As the water rises in a storm, the hero, who tells his adventure in tight first-person narrative, is washed off his precarious rock and hangs over the falls holding to the sheer edge by his hands alone. Actually it turns out that the whole adventure is a dream; but Bird, like Poe interested in psychology, argues that imaginary perils are worse than real ones since imagination is more powerful than reality. The article on Mammoth Cave (first published in two issues of the *American Monthly Magazine* in 1837) is a more usual travel sketch. A competent and imaginative description of the cave and the history of its exploration, it is well spiced with anecdotes. Its main interest is in the fact that it is one of the early accounts of the cave. Even so early the various chambers had received their fanciful names.

II *Uncollected Stories*

Aside from a brief and slightly satiric article on "The Fascinating Power of Reptiles," evidently a lecture of the same sort as that on apparitions, these pieces complete the contents of *Peter Pilgrim.* But notice must be taken of a few short uncollected pieces, published and unpublished. Except for the Indian tale mentioned in connection with the backwoods novels, the sketches in Bird's school composition books are of little interest. Three tales published in the *Philadelphia Monthly Magazine* in 1827 and 1828 are more important. Though its conclusion is weak, the beginning of the ghost story "The Phantom Players," when the hunters run up against a drowned body in the Delaware River, is effective. Much better, indeed a very good ghost story, is

"The Spirit of the Reeds" in which a practical joker pretending to be a ghost pays with his life for rousing the terror of a friend who is crossing a haunted causeway in a howling storm.

Not so effective a story in itself but interesting because of its similarity to *The Narrative of Arthur Gordon Pym, of Nantucket* by Bird's acquaintance Poe, is "The Ice Island," a tale on which Bird's brother Henry collaborated. This is a highly dramatic first-person narrative of a castaway from a shipwreck at sea who finds himself starving, with only a frozen corpse for company, on the horrible dead cold of an iceberg. Bird raises the horror to a high pitch as the fierce seafowls attack the freezing wretch and as the castaway sees a wreck lurch by in the storm, with only a famished dog for crew. But, though its effect is perhaps implied, Bird never uses, as Poe does, the horrifying monotony of whiteness to heighten the horror of desolation. The story thus remains an ordinary account of terrible hardship at sea rather than being raised into an intense drama of psychological significance.

"Adventures in the Wrong House," published in *Godey's Lady's Book* in 1842, is merely a tale version of one of Bird's conventional comic plots. A letter is missent to a virtuous gentleman named James Smith, and he marries at sight a beautiful girl who had been destined for the arms of a villainous James Smith. The incident reminds one of *The City Looking Glass, News of the Night,* and the portion of *Sheppard Lee* dealing with the dandies.

Of Bird's unpublished tales "Awossagame, or the The Seal of the Evil One" is the best. It is an exciting story with an anti-Puritan bias about the Indian girl Awossagame, who is beloved by a tolerant young white man but hated because of her race by the hypocritical Puritans. Accused of witchcraft in Salem and condemned by a stern Puritan judge, she turns out to be the judge's long-lost daughter. Here, as repeatedly throughout his other works, Bird shows he has no use for religiosity. "Death in the Cup" is the result of a request to Bird, much to his amusement since he liked a moderate glass, that he write a temperance story. After several men are nearly hanged or drowned because of drink, they hasten to take the pledge. "Keber Carl" is an unfinished tale of pure melodrama.

III *Non-Fiction*

Robert Montgomery Bird also wrote a great deal of non-fiction, but most of it, like his undistinguished campaign biographies of Major Thomas Stockton and General Zachary Taylor and his numerous able editorials for the Philadelphia *North American,* is not of literary interest. His article in *The Knickerbocker* of 1835 on "Community of Copyright between the United States and Great Britian," however, touches a question vital to the American literature of Bird's time. Bird argues clearly and forcefully that the restriction of American copyright to United States citizens should be repealed and protection given to authors of all nations. To do so would in effect create an international copyright and favor the interests of both American and foreign authors. Interestingly enough, Bird argues not only that American authors ought to be aided but also that justice is due to foreign authors. Bird's article, the only published part of a longer work on copyright that was to include his comments on dramatic copyright (a subject about which he had bitter memories), made such a stir that in the following year Harriet Martineau asked for his help in presenting a petition on copyright to Congress in behalf of a group of British authors.

Two other works of non-fiction are his review of James Montgomery's lectures on literature and poetry (*American Monthly Magazine,* 1834), in which Bird expresses his theories of poetry, and his series of three articles on the Delaware Water Gap in the *North American* in 1853. Undoubtedly, meticulous bibliographical research could identify other works by Bird in periodicals. The student of Bird is tempted, for instance, to attribute to him the article on "Historical Novels" in the *Philadelphia Monthly Magazine* (February, 1829) since Bird made manuscript notes on the same subject from about the same date.

It remains only to speak of a few more of the many works that Bird planned but never wrote. A dozen or more of these have already been mentioned throughout this study—plays, novels, poems, and descriptive books. Bird's papers contain an

[118]

extraordinary number of detailed lists of projected titles. He was interested, for instance, in compiling a whole series of illustrated books. One of these was to be a series on *Wonders of Science;* another a book on agriculture entitled *The Independent Farmer*. But, as he had indicated when he planned his literary career early in his life, he was particularly interested in writing history. At one time he planned a two-volume work, with maps and plates, on the *History of Discovery in the South Seas. Calavar,* he wrote in the introduction to the edition of 1837, was intended to prepare the way for a history of Mexico. Another scheme was for a *History of the Annexation of Texas and the War with Mexico*. But the plan that came nearest to fruition was for a general history of the United States. For this he collected an enormous amount of bibliography and a mass of notes. Actual publication for the history was arranged in 1839 with Lea and Blanchard, who pressed him for copy in 1840. But Bird became too busy with his farm and later with his medical lecturing and his editorship. The result was that the history was never completed, and we of the present have no real way of knowing whether Bird was truly so profound an historical scholar as his friends frequently asserted.

CHAPTER 10

Conclusion

TO HIS CONTEMPORARIES Robert Montgomery Bird
seemed a writer of major stature. It is true that Sydney George
Fisher interjects a word of opposition: "I know Bird very well, he
has talents, but of a second rate order. His imagination is not
sustained, strengthened and regulated by intellect and his mind
is uncultivated. His novels were failures, and his plays, tho
containing some poetic and well written passages, have been
deservedly damned, with faint praise."[1] But Fisher's sour comment does not represent the usual accolade which Bird received.
He was sought after as a judge for literary contests. He was invited to undertake the editorship of periodicals. His poems and
stories were anthologized. His dramas were some of the most
popular American tragedies on the stage of his time, and Forrest
made *The Gladiator* one of the all-time successes of the American
theater. As a novelist he received repeated acclaim. His novels
were consistently pirated not by one but by two British publishers. In America James Rees placed him "in the front rank
of American novelists" and, in what was in those days very high
praise indeed, said that *Nick of the Woods* was superior to any
one of Bulwer's novels and a compliment to the literature of our
country.[2] A reviewer in the *Western Monthly Magazine* (January,
1835) called *Calavar* "decidedly the best American novel that
has been written" except for Cooper's novels of the sea. Bird
was more usually, however, compared with John Pendleton
Kennedy and William Gilmore Simms, to both of whom he was
generally thought equal or superior.

I *Poet and Dramatist*

How true this praise rings today is debatable. As a poet Bird
can certainly be dismissed. Neither the sentimental lyrics popular in his day nor the grandiose philosophical allegories of the

unfinished poem "The Cave" seem now to have any real value. Aside from the editorials, which must be judged by another standard, there is not enough prose non-fiction by Bird for us clearly to assess his capabilities in this field. He himself felt that his talents did not lie in the direction of periodical writing: "I am entirely of too discursive and diffuse a turn," he wrote to Samuel Gridley Howe in 1834, "to shine in a nutshell. . . . I have always been more disposed to count by *Acts* and *Chapters*, than by lines and paragraphs."[3] It is true that the articles on Mammoth Cave have attained some celebrity, but their value is greater as early accounts of cave exploration than as literary productions.

Concerning Bird's drama there is more room for debate. Arthur Hobson Quinn has praised it highly—much too highly, in my opinion. He has praised Bird as a writer of tragedy for his "rare sense of dramatic effect, a power to visualize historic scenes and characters, to seize the spirit of the past out of the mass of facts and, in a few brief lines, to fuse those facts into life." "Before he was thirty years old," Quinn writes of Bird, "he had lifted romantic tragedy to a level higher than it had reached in England since Congreve."[4] Quinn praises even several of the never acted comedies.

Such criticism seems to me the reaction of a tired traveler seeking the shadow of any small rock within an inordinately weary land. For though Bird is undoubtedly the best of the Philadelphia dramatic group of his time, the general level of American drama in the early nineteenth century is so low that his pre-eminence counts for little. His comedies, certainly, are derivative, overwritten, with no real human interest and no real characters. His tragedies provide scope for brilliant pageantry and set scenes. Many of the speeches are excellent rhetoric; they have been deservedly popular as elocutionary pieces for recitation. But the themes of the tragedies are overstated, the characters unreal, and the situations overdramatized. In them no deep substratum of thought or understanding of human nature is evident. Bird does, however, deserve credit for his skill in writing dramas so precisely adapted to the theatrical requirements and preferences of the day and to the special capabilities of Edwin Forrest. Quinn may possibly be right that, given better conditions in the theater and a greater encouragement for the dramatist, Bird might have developed into a first-rate dramatic author. Unfortunately the fact is that, though he was successful in writing for the theater, Bird did not break far enough away from the inhibiting conventions of his time to write drama of lasting literary value.

II *Novelist*

Bird must, then, stand or fall with his novels. Much redounds to his credit. In a day when Young America was preaching a strict nationalism of theme, he stood out stoutly for the novelist's right to treat subjects of general rather than of merely national interest. He opened up for American novelists the romance of ancient Mexico. In his romances like *Calavar* he is excellent in summoning up the pageantry of history; his set descriptions are often striking. In *Nick of the Woods* and to a certain extent in *The Hawks of Hawk Hollow,* he successfully casts over his main characters—Nathan Slaughter and Oran Gilbert, respectively—an aura of mysterious legend that makes them become almost mythic figures. In *Nick* particularly there are many exciting episodes of rapid action. Bird the novelist (as I have said earlier) did not forget his apprenticeship as dramatist. Scene after scene in all the books, even in hurried *Robin Day,* is sharply visualized for the reader.

In addition, Bird has a fund of ironic humor. As he grows older, he moves away from romantic sentiment and nobility toward a realistic record, with satiric overtones, of American life. The "Western" humor of Captain Stackpole in *Nick* is a beginning, but the sharp ironic comment for which Bird had a real talent is best observed in *Sheppard Lee,* parts of *Robin Day,* and a few of the shorter tales. With this increase of interest in the humorous and satiric comes a corresponding improvement of style. From the ponderous archaism of the Mexican romances he progresses to the intentionally more simple style of *The Hawks* and to the clear and easy styles of *Sheppard Lee.* He particularly improves his ability to write dialect. Unlike his knights of the Conquest, his Stackpoles and Slaughters and Gilberts speak convincingly; and *Sheppard Lee,* a minor *tour de force* in its variation from style to style, maintains realism in language. In *Sheppard Lee,* indeed, Bird, after having written with considerable success the bloodcurdling romance of flight and pursuit in the backwoods, is moving toward a more sophisticated novel of psychological analysis and of ironic social satire. We regret that he did not proceed further in this direction and that, writing in sickness and led astray by a facility for romantic plot-weaving, he lost control of *Robin Day*.

Against these very real credits—*Nick of the Woods* can stand up well against any novel by Cooper—there are unfortunately debits. Many of these are the results of Bird's following the literary conventions of his time; others spring from his personal theories of fiction. In his historical novels, following Scott and the tradition of Scott, Bird attempts to recount historical events accurately and to weave around them a fictional story involving only a few of the historical characters. But since, unlike Scott's, his fictional characters are not truly representative of historical facts, and since (especially in the Mexican novels) his plots are conventions from Gothic romance, the two parts of his books do not join in effective unity. We would like to separate them. When enjoying the vivid account of the Conquest of Mexico, we become impatient with mad knights, disguised maidens, and vengeful Moors. Yet in another kind of book such figures might have a logical place, and Bird does indeed show much ingenuity in reweaving the old Gothic tapestries. Bird, who was interested in the theory as well as the practice of historical fiction, was never able to solve the problem of joining the fictional to the historical. The fictional story often seems an excrescence awkwardly worked into the historical picture.

Closely related to Bird's refusal to make the historical heroes his fictional heroes is his largely conventional but partly theoretical preference for a weak, too noble, too self-sacrificing upper-class hero. In choosing such a romantic hero, he is, of course, following Scott and Cooper and many other authors of his time. But those authors frequently push their romantic heroes into the background. Bird, in *The Hawks* and *Nick*, keeps his annoyingly in the foreground. Theoretically it ought to be better practice to do so, but it does not seem to be. Hyland Gilbert, for instance, merely gets in the way of the fascinating outlaw Oran. We really wish he would either become a bold outlaw himself or would die of his sickly idealism. Yet such is the hero that Bird chose on definite theoretical grounds. Answering a critical letter from James Lawson about *The Infidel,* Bird wrote:

> The character of Juan I meant to be "passive". . . . You certainly are wrong about the "action, action, action" being as necessary in a novel as in a play. The deepest interest can be drawn from the sufferings of individuals incapable of resisting their fate, and even when they attempt no resistance. Such is found in *The Bride of Lammermoor,* where the heroine is wax and the hero lead, clay, water, or anything. And that fiction, if you will take my word for it, is the most interesting and deeply affecting ever penned by the hand of man. The actors do nothing; but how one's tears drop over them;—nay over their memory.[5]

Meekly suffering heroes are not, it seems to me, to the modern taste, especially in books of violent adventure. We are relieved when Robin Day, though against his will, often does act the *picaro* or villain. In *Sheppard Lee* Bird cleverly solves the problem of the active and inactive hero through his device of having the essentially good and passive Lee transformed, though without complete loss of his original individuality, into a series of various characters, several of whom are capable of real action. It must be said, however, that in general Bird is unable to create rounded, realistic characters. In the romantic novels characters such as Oran and Nathan and Stackpole, and perhaps even Cortez, are more legendary types than actual persons; in the satiric books the individual characters are representative of social groups.

However, much of the weakness in Bird's novels goes back to his theory of the novel. At the beginning of his career, at least, he had no idea of the need in a novel for strong, unified structure. The novelist, he thought, need not work nearly so hard as the dramatist. "Novels" he wrote in his *Secret Records,*

> are much easier sorts of things [than plays], and immortalize one's pocket much sooner. . . . How blessedly and lazily, in making a novel, a man may go spinning and snoring over his quires! here scribbling acres of fine vapid dialogue, and there scrawling out regions of descriptions about roses and old weather-beaten houses. I think I could manufacture a novel every quarter. But to be set down with the asses who are doing these sort of things; and a hundred years hence, have my memory covered

in three lines of Biographical Dictionary, as one of the herd of liars of the last century! I had sooner be pickled with navy pork, and eaten as soon as I was preserved. . . . [A] dramatist deserves honour far above a romancer—any thing Mr. Godwin says to the contrary notwithstanding; and the qualities necessary to one who would write a first-rate play would, if concentered in one individual, make him almost a god.[6]

"A Novel," he says in the introduction to *The Hawks,* "is, at best, a piece of Mosaic-work, of which the materials have been scraped up here or there, sometimes from the forgotten tablets of a predecessor, sometimes from the decaying pillars of history, sometimes from the little mine of precious stones that is found in the human brain. . . ." Elsewhere he compares a novel to an avalanche that, started with a few stones, at last comes thundering down the mountainside.

None of these comments indicates care for the careful work of shaping and moulding a novel according to a tight preordained plan; all emphasize spontaneity and almost carelessness of writing. Poe was right when, pretending to deduce his conclusion from Bird's handwritten signature, he said that Bird had vivid imagination but also a tendency toward "an uneasy want of finish."[7] From these faults, indeed, Bird's novels do suffer. The masses of truly excellent material are not well enough digested into choate order; the parts are better than the wholes. In many of the books, as certainly in *Robin Day,* there is too much material; more selection should have been exercised. *Nick of the Woods* would not suffer from condensation and simplification, especially in the story of the wicked Braxley; had the superfluous been cut away, the fascinating character of Nathan and the thrilling adventures would have stood out in higher relief. What Bird could have done with better control is indicated by *Sheppard Lee.* There, disciplined strictly by his own scheme (artificial though it may be), Bird achieves a stronger effect in a relatively short book than he does in most of his longer ones.

III *Representative of a Literary Era*

Though Robert Montgomery Bird cannot claim the laurels of a first-rate author, he is historically important if only because, in an era of American literature when such achievement was unusual, he had written by the time of his death four major tragedies and fourteen volumes of prose fiction, not to mention a number of poems and articles and a great mass of political comment. Without doubt he was the outstanding man of letters in Philadelphia of his period and the true successor in the novel of his fellow Philadelphian Charles Brockden Brown.[8] For a few richly productive years, from 1831 through 1836, he was certainly one of the most fertile and influential of American authors.

Moreover, partly because he seldom could rise above the mediocre conventions of his era, Robert Montgomery Bird is a fascinating figure to the historian of American literature. His life and works paint a clearer and broader picture of the literary scene than those of almost any other author of the time. *The Gladiator* and *The Broker of Bogota,* and to a lesser extent *Oralloossa* and *Pelopidas,* show the kind of tragedy that appealed to the audiences of the early nineteenth century. Bird's association with Edwin Forrest gives an insight into the relationships in America between actor and writer, in the same way that Bulwer's association with Macready does in England. Bird's romances, even in their faults, demonstrate clearly the tastes of the writers of the American novel during this period. Here are the historical backgrounds, exciting suspenseful adventures, vivid minor characters, pallid and annoying heroes and heroines, and stilted moralizing that characterize much of Cooper and Simms and even of Hawthorne and Melville. Here, too, is the urgent desire to make use of American materials and American scenes, whether in the plains and mountains of Mexico or in the wilderness of Kentucky and the Delaware Water Gap. Furthermore, Bird's myriad literary schemes and his almost wholly unprofitable career as a man of letters in Philadelphia, then the home of a renowned school of tragic dramatists and the center of much of America's literary activity, graphically exemplify the hopes and successes and failures that faced an American author of the 1830's and 1840's.

Bird is also a fascinating study in growth and change. Though his literary career was very short, really extending only from 1829 to 1839, one can see shadowed in it the changes in American literary attitudes in a crucial decade. From prolix and inflated style he moves toward simplicity. From melodramatic tragedy set in foreign lands and times long ago, he moves in *The Broker of Bogota* toward more domestic and modern tragedy. He then turns away from verse tragedy to the romance, and finally (if one accepts Hawthorne's distinction) to the novel. From Gothic tales of the Spaniards in Mexico he turns to traditions of the American Revolution and legends of Indian atrocities in the Bloody Ground of Kentucky. Then, in what is certainly one of his best books, he turns in *Sheppard Lee* to satiric social comment on his own America. And though *Robin Day* degenerates into a bare recital of impossible adventures, it, too, evidently began as a picaresque novel of social comment.

Robert Montgomery Bird must remain, then, a minor author. With no strong original literary theories or conceptions and with no strikingly new or profound things to say he cannot claim literary pre-eminence. His tragedies, though two of them gained great success on the nineteenth-century stage, to the modern reader seem strained and melodramatic. His comedies are derivative and, on the whole, unfunny. Since Bird never completed the extensive historical works he planned, the critic cannot judge him by these. Though his prose sketches have considerable charm and humor, they are written in a ponderous and self-conscious style unpopular today. His poetry, well calculated to please the taste of early nineteenth-century readers of polite magazines and sentimental anthologies, seems now (to say the best of it) mediocre. His novels of the conquest of Mexico, despite their rich and vivid historical tableaux, are stilted and unreal. In his novels of the frontier, exciting though they be, and in his often fascinating stories of abnormal psychology, Bird cannot match the sustained genius of Cooper on the one hand nor of Poe on the other. His works are mainly important because of the particularly illuminating insight they give into salient trends in literary history. Yet despite their lack of high literary stature, the best writings of Robert Montgomery Bird can still afford abundant pleasure to the reader who enjoys a lofty drama of human freedom, a stirring tale of adventure in the American backwoods, or a piquant and amusing satire on ridiculous aspects of nineteenth-century American society.

Notes and References

Note: It has seemed unnecessary to annotate every statement of fact. Biographical and bibliographical facts are drawn, usually with no acknowledgment, either from manuscript materials in the Bird Collection at the University of Pennsylvania or from works of the following authors listed in the last section of my bibliography: Mary Mayer Bird, Clement E. Foust, A. H. Quinn, James Rees, C. Seymour Thompson, and Cecil B. Williams. Williams' introduction and notes to *Nick of the Woods* have been very helpful. Only certain specific debts are acknowledged in these footnotes.

Chapter One

1. Arthur Hobson Quinn, "Robert Montgomery Bird," *Dictionary of American Biography,* II, 287-88. See also James Rees, *The Life of Edwin Forrest* (Philadelphia, 1874), pp. 425-26.

2. See Richard Harris, "A Young Dramatist's Diary: *The Secret Records* of R. M. Bird," University of Pennsylvania *Library Chronicle,* XXV (Winter, 1959), 9-10.

3. See Hervey Allen, *Israfel: The Life and Times of Edgar Allan Poe* (2 vols.; New York, 1926), II, 574.

4. For a study and assessment of Bird as newspaper editor see Robert L. Bloom, "Robert Montgomery Bird, Editor," *Pennsylvania Magazine of History and Biography,* LXXVI (April, 1952), 123-41.

5. According to his passport of 1833, Bird was about five feet eleven inches tall, with a high forehead, light eyes, ordinary nose and mouth but rather large chin, fair complexion, and full face.

Chapter Two

1. "To Lyce," *Philadelphia Monthly Magazine,* I (August, 1828), 303-4.

2. "Saul's Last Day," *The Philadelphia Book* (Philadelphia, 1836), pp. 147-50.

3. "Theatrical Address," *Philadelphia Monthly Magazine,* II (November, 1828), 63-64.

4. Printed in Mary Mayer Bird, *Life of Robert Montgomery Bird,* ed. C. Seymour Thompson (Philadelphia, 1945), p. 45.

5. *The Young Lady's Book of Elegant Poetry* (Philadelphia, 1836), p. 153. I have emended "the" to "thy" in the first line of the quotation.

6. Manuscript introduction to "The Cave" in the Bird Collection.

Chapter Three

1. Arthur Hobson Quinn in *The Literature of the American People*, ed. A. H. Quinn *et al.* (New York, 1951), p. 474.
2. See Richard Harris, "From the Papers of R. M. Bird: The Last Scene from *News of the Night*," University of Pennsylvania *Library Chronicle*, XXIV (Winter, 1958), 1-12.
3. Information on this and other recent productions of Bird's plays can be found in A. H. Quinn's introduction to *The City Looking Glass* (New York, 1933) and Quinn's other studies of Bird as a dramatist.
4. *Literature of the American People*, p. 474.

Chapter Four

1. Richard Moody, *Edwin Forrest, First Star of the American Stage* (New York, 1960), pp. 90-91.
2. See Richard Harris, "A Young Dramatist's Diary: *The Secret Records* of R. M. Bird," University of Pennsylvania *Library Chronicle*, XXV (Winter, 1959), 9-10.
3. The best account of American drama of this period is found in Arthur Hobson Quinn, *A History of American Drama from the Beginning to the Civil War* (New York, 1923).
4. Clement E. Foust, *The Life and Dramatic Works of Robert Montgomery Bird* (New York, 1919), pp. 73-74.
5. *The Fabulous Forrest* (Boston, 1929), pp. 100-1.
6. Foust, pp. 37-38.
7. See Harris, "A Young Dramatist's Diary," pp. 12-13 and notes on p. 22.
8. Francis Courtney Wemyss, *Twenty-six Years of the Life of an Actor and Manager* (2 vols.; New York, 1847), I, 194.
9. Quinn, *The Literature of the American People*, p. 477.
10. Moses, p. 101.
11. Rees, p. 100.
12. See my "Bulwer-Lytton and the School of Catastrophe," *Philological Quarterly*, XXXII (October, 1953), 428-42; "The American School of Catastrophe," *American Quarterly*, XI (Fall, 1959), 380-90; and "Recreators of Pompeii," *Archaeology*, IX (Autumn, 1956), 182-91. Bird was to re-use the theme in his novel *The Infidel*.
13. "*The Gladiator*—Mr. Forrest—Acting," *The Brooklyn Eagle*, December 26, 1846, as reprinted in Montrose J. Moses and John Mason Brown, *The American Theatre as Seen by Its Critics, 1752-1934* (New York, 1934), p. 69. It is a play, Whitman continues, "calculated to make the hearts of the masses swell responsively to

. . . nobler, manlier aspirations in behalf of mortal freedom."

14. Harris, "A Young Dramatist's Diary," pp. 10, 17.

15. Letter of April 10, 1832.

16. Quoted in Mary Mayer Bird, p. 55.

17. *Literature of the American People*, p. 476.

Chapter Five

1. My information both in this chapter and in Chapter VII about dramas and novels on the subject of American Indians is in large part drawn from Albert Keiser, *The Indian in American Literature* (New York, 1933). For Indian drama see also Laurence Hutton, *Curiosities of the American Stage* (New York, 1891), pp. 8-18; Quinn, *History of American Drama*, pp. 269-75; and Arthur Hornblow, *A History of the Theatre in America from Its Beginnings to the Present Time* (2 vols.; Philadelphia, 1919), II, 61.

2. Keiser, p. 94.

3. Letter of April 10, 1832.

4. Quoted in Foust, p. 53.

5. Rees, p. 100.

6. *Literature of the American People*, p. 479.

7. *The Life of Edwin Forrest, The American Tragedian* (2 vols.; Philadelphia, 1877), I, 353.

8. "The Diaries of Sydney George Fisher 1837-1838," *Pennsylvania Magazine of History and Biography*, LXXVI (July, 1952), 332.

9. *A Short History of the American Drama* (New York, 1932), p. 102.

10. Hornblow, p. 62. Compare Rees, p. 423, and *American Quarterly Review* (Philadelphia), XVI (December, 1834), 375-401.

11. Harris, "A Young Dramatist's Diary," p. 17.

12. *Ibid.*, p. 16.

13. Foust, p. 75.

Chapter Six

1. This novel is not to be confused with the story of the same title which was to be set in the American Revolution and to include an account of the Battle of the Brandywine.

2. Review of *Calavar* in the *Literary Gazette* (London), June 13, 1835, p. 374.

3. Review of *Calavar* in the "Editor's Table" of *The Knickerbocker*, IV (October, 1834), 324.

4. Book V, Chapter II.

5. Review of *The Hawks of Hawk Hollow*.

6. See citations in n. 12 of Chap. IV above.

Chapter Seven

1. Letter printed in "An Itinerant Portrait Painter," University of Pennsylvania *Library Chronicle,* XIII (December, 1945), 126.
2. *Ibid.,* p. 125. See also pp. 100, 106.
3. March 12, 1836, pp. 189-90.
4. For a meticulous and highly illuminating study of Bird's sources see pp. xxxvi-xl of Williams' introduction. I rely heavily on Williams.
5. Quoted in Mary Mayer Bird, p. 70.
6. See Harold H. Scudder, "Bartram's 'Travels': A Note on the Use of Bartram's 'Travels' by the Author of 'Nick of the Woods,'" *Notes and Queries,* CLXXXIV (March 13, 1943), 154-55.
7. *The Prose Writers of America,* 4th ed. rev. (Philadelphia, 1859), p. 435.
8. Quoted in Mary Mayer Bird, p. 63.
9. Francis Parkman, *The Conspiracy of Pontiac,* Frontenac Edition (2 vols.; Boston, 1889), II, 127.
10. (3 vols.; New York, 1930), II, 191-92.

Chapter Eight

1. Originally published in *Southern Literary Messenger,* II (September, 1836), 662-67.
2. See Killis Campbell, "The Source of Poe's 'Some Words with a Mummy,'" *Nation,* XC (June 23, 1910), 625-26, and *idem, The Mind of Poe* (Cambridge, Mass., 1933), p. 172.

[No notes to *Chapter Nine*]

Chapter Ten

1. Fisher, p. 332.
2. Rees, pp. 424-25.
3. Quoted in slightly different form in Foust, pp. 112-13.
4. *Literature of the American People,* p. 482.
5. Foust, p. 87.
6. Harris, "A Young Dramatist's Diary," p. 17.
7. See the comment on Bird in "A Chapter on Autography."
8. According to Vernon Louis Parrington in *Main Currents,* II, 191, he was "probably the ablest man of letters that Philadelphia produced" in his day. Ellis Paxson Oberholtzer in *The Literary History of Philadelphia* (Philadelphia, 1906) p. 268, calls him the man on whom the literary claims of Philadelphia in that era must rest.

Selected Bibliography

The intention of the following bibliography is to list all literary publications by Robert Montgomery Bird and a selected number of books and articles about him. I have not tried to identify his many editorials, largely on politics, in the Philadelphia *North American* during the years when he was its editor. The names of publishers are listed only when they seem of particular bibliographical interest. Acknowledgment is hereby given of great indebtedness to the bibliographies of Joseph Sabin, Jacob Blanck, Clement E. Foust, and Cecil B. Williams. However, for Foust's attribution to Bird of three poems in the *Philadelphia Monthly Magazine*—"The Dead Soldier" (November, 1827), "Summer" (August, 1828), and "The Helots" (September, 1828)—I can discover no justifying evidence. The first of the three poems is certainly by Bird's brother Henry. A bibliographical complexity is also provided by the poem "Saul's Last Day" listed by Foust as appearing in the same periodical in October, 1827. In the original state of the October, 1827, issue Bird's poem did not appear, but that issue was recalled and reprinted in December with Bird's poem substituted for another poem. The reason is not clear. None of Bird's dramas was published during his lifetime nor for some time afterwards, since Edwin Forrest, who held the manuscripts, refused permission.

PRIMARY SOURCES

I. *Separate Publications by R. M. Bird*

God Bless America. National Hymn Written and Composed with Accompaniment for the Piano Forte by Robert M. Bird. Philadelphia: Fiot, Meignen and Co., 1834 [sheet music]. Reprinted in *American Melodies*. Ed. George P. Morris. New York, 1840, pp. 114-16.

Calavar; or, The Knight of the Conquest: A Romance of Mexico. Philadelphia: Carey, Lea and Blanchard, 1834. 2 vols. [same], 1835.

    Abdalla the Moor, and the Spanish Knight. London: A. K. Newman, 1835. 4 vols.

    Calavar; or, The Knight of the Conquest . . . . Philadelphia: Carey, Lea and Blanchard, 1837. 2 vols.

Abdalla the Moor and the Spanish Knight. A Romance of Mexico. London: J. Cunningham, 1839.

Calavar; or, The Knight of the Conquest . . . . New edition. Philadelphia: Lea and Blanchard, 1847. 2 vols.

[same], 3rd edition. Illus. by F. O. C. Darley. New York: J. S. Redfield, 1854.

[same], Nos. 24 and 25 in Dürr's Collection of Standard American Authors. Leipzig [between 1854 and 1858].

[same]. New York, 1864.

Calavar, The Knight of the Conquest. Illus. New York: W. J. Widdleton, 1876.

The Infidel; or, The Fall of Mexico. A Romance. Philadelphia: Carey, Lea and Blanchard, 1835. 2 vols.

[same], 2nd edition, 1835.

Cortes: or The Fall of Mexico. London: Richard Bentley, 1835. 3 vols.

The Infidel's Doom; or, Cortes and the Conquest of Mexico. London: J. Cunningham, 1840.

The Hawks of Hawk-Hollow. A Tradition of Pennsylvania. Philadelphia: Carey, Lea and Blanchard, 1835. 2 vols.

[same]. 2nd edition, Philadelphia, 1835. 2 vols.

[same]. London: A. K. Newman, 1837. 2 vols.

[same]. London: J. Cunningham, 1839.

[same]. London: N. Bruce, 1842.

[same]. London: Ward and Lock, 1856.

Sheppard Lee. Written by Himself. New York: Harper and Bros., 1836. 2 vols. [Published anonymously.]

Nick of the Woods, or The Jibbenainosay. A Tale of Kentucky. Philadelphia: Carey, Lea and Blanchard, 1837. 2 vols.

Nick of the Woods; A Story of Kentucky. Ed. W. Harrison Ainsworth. London: Richard Bentley, 1837. 3 vols.

[same]. London, 1841.

Nick of the Woods. London: J. S. Pratt, 1845.

Nick of the Woods; or, The Jibbenainosay; A Tale of Kentucky. A new edition, revised by the author. New York: J. S. Redfield, 1853.

[same]. 1854.

Nick of the Woods; or, Adventures of Prairie Life. London: Ward and Lock, 1854.

[same]. Halifax, 1855.

[same]. 4th edition, London, 1856.

[same]. London, 1860.

Nick of the Woods; or, The Jibbenainosay. A Tale of Kentucky. New York: W. J. Widdleton, 1864.

The History of Nick of the Woods; the Jibbenainosay; the Wandering Demon of the Forest, and the Howl of the Red Man. New York: Turner and Fisher [Only thirty-six pages: evidently a drastic condensation. Undated, but probably in the 1860's].

Nick of the Woods; or, Adventures of Prairie Life. London: Routledge, 1872.

Nick of the Woods; or, The Jibbenainosay. New York: W. J. Widdleton, 1876.

[same]. New York: A. C. Armstrong and Son, 1881.

[same]. London, 1883.

[same]. 1884.

[same]. New York, 1890.

Nick of the Woods. New York: Burrows, 1904.

Nick of the Woods: A Story of the Early Settlers in Kentucky. Illus. by J. W. Davis. New York: A. L. Burt, n.d. [1905?].

Nick of the Woods; or, Adventures of Prairie Life. London: W. Nicholson and Son, n.d.

Nick of the Woods or The Jibbenainosay. A Tale of Kentucky. New York: John W. Lovell, n.d.

[same]. No. 5 in *An American Bookshelf*, ed. Mark Van Doren. New York: Vanguard Press, Macy-Masius, 1928.

Nick of the Woods . . . . Ed. with introduction, chronology, and bibliography by Cecil B. Williams. New York: American Book Company, 1939. [The best edition. Includes a careful historical and biographical introduction, a full bibliography, and illuminating maps. Indispensable for a full study of the book.]

Nick of the Woods . . . . Adapted for modern readers by Marshall McClintock. Illus. by Thomas Fogarty, Jr. New York: Vanguard Press, 1941.

Peter Pilgrim: or, A Rambler's Recollections. Philadelphia: Lea and Blanchard, 1838. 2 vols.

[same]. London: J. Cunningham, 1838.

Peter Pilgrim, A Tale. London: R. Bentley, 1839. 2 vols.

(*Peter Pilgrim; or, A Rambler's Recollections,* Philadelphia: Lea and Blanchard, 1838. Nineteenth Century American Literature on Microcards. Series A, The Ohio Valley. Louisville, Kentucky: Lost Cause Press, 1956.)

The Adventures of Robin Day. Philadelphia: Lea and Blanchard, 1839. 2 vols.

Robin Day; or, The Rover's Life. London: J. Cunningham, 1840.

The Adventures of Robin Day. New York: J. Polhemus, 1877.

Selected Bibliography

*The Difficulties of Medical Science. An Inaugural Lecture Intro-
ductory to a Course of Lectures.* Philadelphia, 1841.
*Valedictory Address Delivered before the Graduates of Pennsylvania
Medical College, Session of 1842-3.* Philadelphia, 1843.
*Sketch of the Life, Public Services, and Character of Major Thomas
Stockton of New-Castle, The Candidate of the Whig Party for
the Office of Governor of Delaware.* Wilmington, Delaware, 1844.
*A Brief Review of the Career, Character & Campaigns of Zachary
Taylor.* Washington, D.C., 1848. [Identifiable as Bird's by men-
tion in his correspondence with Senator Clayton.]
The City Looking Glass. A Philadelphia Comedy. Ed. Arthur Hobson
Quinn. New York, 1933.
The Cowled Lover and Other Plays, Ed. Edward H. O'Neill. Vol.
XII in *America's Lost Plays,* ed. Barrett H. Clark, Princeton, 1941.

II. *Translations of Bird's Works*

Calavar, der Ritter der Eroberung. Ein Roman aus Mexico. Tr. G. N.
Bärmann. Schneeberg, 1836.
Calavar, oder der Ritter der Eroberung. Ein Roman aus Mexico.
Tr. Wilhelm Weber. St. Louis, 1848.
Die Falken aus der Falken-Höhle. Eine Geschichte aus Pensylvanien.
Included in Klassicher Schriftsteller Nordamerikas: Ausgewählte
Amerikanische Romane. Frankfort, 1840.
De valken uit het valkenhol. Eene geschiedenis uit Pensylvanië.
Deventer, 1843. 2 vols.
Nathan der Quaker, oder der Satan des Urwaldes. Tr. Johann
Sporschil. Leipzig, 1838. 3 vols.
Der Waldteufel. Ein Roman aus Kentucky. Included in Ausgewählte
Amerikanische Romane. Frankfort, 1841.
Die Gefahren der Wildnis. Eine Erzählung für die reifere Jugend.
Tr. Franz Hoffman. Illus. Stuttgart, 1847. (Other editions in
1875 and 1891.)
Skovdjævelen. Fortælling af det amerikaniske Colonistliv. Copen-
hagen, 1847-50.
Puscios duasia. Puikus apsakymas is Amerikanisku misku. Tr. W. L.
Ancyc. Chicago, 1905.
Duch puszczy; opowiadanie zborów amerykańskich według d-ra Birda.
Tr. Władysław Ludwik Anczyc. 7th ed. Warsaw, n.d.
*Jibbenainosay; Roland Forrester och hans kusin Edits underbara
äventyr Nordamerikas Indianer.* Tr. L. Arosenius. Stockholm,
1912.
(A Dutch edition was published in Leyden in 1877)
Robin Dey oder das Leben eines Unglücksvogels. Tr. W. E. Drugulin.
Leipzig [between 1853 and 1858].

III. *Works in Periodicals and Anthologies*

"Translation from Horace," *Philadelphia Monthly Magazine*, October, 1827.

"Saul's Last Day," *Philadelphia Monthly Magazine*, October, 1827. [See headnote to Bibliography.] Reprinted in *The Philadelphia Book; or Specimens of Metropolitan Literature*. Philadelphia, 1836, pp. 147-50.

"The Dying Bride," *Philadelphia Monthly Magazine*, November, 1827.

"The Miniature," *Philadelphia Monthly Magazine*, November, 1827.

"The Death of Meleager," *Philadelphia Monthly Magazine*, December, 1827.

"The Ice Island," *Philadelphia Monthly Magazine*, December, 1827. [Partly by Henry D. Bird.] Reprinted in *The Philadelphia Book*, pp. 264-74.

"Rest in Thine Isle, Young Hero, Rest" song, *Philadelphia Monthly Magazine*, December, 1827.

"The Spirit of the Reeds," *Philadelphia Monthly Magazine*, January, 1828.

"Friendship," *Philadelphia Monthly Magazine*, January, 1828.

"The Phantom Players," *Philadelphia Monthly Magazine*, May, 1828.

"Changing Heart, Away from Me" song, *Philadelphia Monthly Magazine*, July, 1828.

"Brunette," *Philadelphia Monthly Magazine*, August, 1828.

"To Lyce," *Philadelphia Monthly Magazine*, August, 1828 [translation from Horace].

"The Love Sick Minstrel" song, *Philadelphia Monthly Magazine*, September, 1828.

"Great Shakespeare Tells Us: Address for the Opening of a New Theater," *Philadelphia Monthly Magazine*, November, 1828.

"She Opes her Eyes and Oh My Bosom's Swell," *New York Mirror*, May, 1832.

"Mary," *New York Mirror*, May 12, 1832.

Review of James Montgomery's *Lectures on General Literature, Poetry*, etc., *American Monthly Magazine*, February, 1834.

"The Beech Tree," *New York Mirror*, March, 1834. Reprinted in *The Atlantic Club-Book: Being Sketches in Prose and Verse, by Various Authors*. 2 vols. New York, 1834, II, 268-69.

"The China Tree," *Knickerbocker Magazine*, January, 1835. Reprinted in *The Young Lady's Book of Elegant Poetry*. Philadelphia, 1835, pp. 152-53.

"An Evening Ode," *Knickerbocker*, February, 1835. Reprinted as "Ode O Melancholy Moon" in *The Young Lady's Book*, pp. 142-43.

Selected Bibliography

"To Governor M'Duffie," *New England Magazine*, February, 1835.
"Community of Copyright between the United States and Great Britain," *Knickerbocker*, October, 1835.
"Romance of Cid Ramon," *The Young Lady's Book*, pp. 269-72 [Reprinted from *Calavar*].
"To a Child," *The Young Man's Book of Elegant Poetry*. Philadelphia, 1835, p. 113.
"To an Old Sycamore, On the Banks of the Ohio," *The Young Man's Book*, pp. 168-71. [Written for the Buckeyes' celebration of the 47th anniversary of the landing at the mouth of the Muskingum River, Ohio, April, 1385.]
"Address . . . at the Wood Complimentary Benefit," *National Gazette*, January 11, 1836.
"Lament," *United States Gazette*, April, 1837.
"Adventures in the Wrong House," *Godey's Lady's Book*, December, 1842. Reprinted in the *Germantown Telegraph*, December 3 and 10, 1856.
"The Mammoth Cave of Kentucky," *American Monthly Magazine*, May and June, 1837. Reprinted in *Peter Pilgrim*.
"A Tale of a Snag," *American Monthly Magazine*, August, 1837. Also in *The Spirit of the Times*, August 12, 1837. Reprinted in *Peter Pilgrim*.
"Letters from the Gap," Philadelphia *North American*, August 10, 25, and September 2, 1853.
"Serenade," *The Book of Rubies: A Collection of the Most Notable Love-Poems in the English Language*. New York, 1866, pp. 240-41. This volume was reissued in 1874 as *Half Hours with the Poets*.
"A Belated Revenge. From the Papers of Ipsico Poe," *Lippincott's Monthly Magazine*, November, 1889. [Edited and completed by Frederick Mayer Bird.]
The Broker of Bogota. Included in *Representative American Plays*. Ed. A. H. Quinn. New York, 1917, pp. 209-51.
Pelopidas, The Gladiator, Oralloossa, and *The Broker of Bogota*: see Foust, Clement E. among Secondary Sources of this bibliography.
The City Looking Glass. Included in *The Colophon*, New York, 1933. [Edited A. H. Quinn.] Published also as a separate volume.
The Gladiator. Included in *American Plays*. Ed. A. G. Halline. New York, 1935, pp. 153-98.

IV. *Dramatizations of the Novels*

HAINES, J. T. *Nick of the Woods; or, The Altar of Revenge*. London, n.d. No. 352 of Duncombe's Acting Editions. First produced in 1839.

MEDINA, LOUISA H. *Nick of the Woods. A Drama in Three Acts.* Boston, 1856. No. LXII of Spencer's Boston Theatre. Reprinted in French's Standard Drama. New York [1864]. See below.

[MEDINA, LOUISA H.] *Nick of the Woods; or, Telie, the Renegade's Daughter. An Old Melodrama in Three Acts with Music; Adapted by Tom Taggart.* New York: Samuel French, 1940.

(BENJAMIN H. BREWSTER dramatized *The Infidel* in 1835)

SECONDARY SOURCES

BIRD, MARY MAYER. *Life of Robert Montgomery Bird.* Ed. C. Seymour Thompson. Philadelphia: University of Pennsylvania Library, 1945. Reprinted from the University of Pennsylvania *Library Chronicle.* Includes selections from Bird's correspondence and early poems. A basic source.

BLANCK, JACOB. "Robert Montgomery Bird," *Bibliography of American Literature.* New Haven: Yale University Press, 1955. I, 228-34. The most complete technical bibliography.

BLOOM, ROBERT L. "Robert Montgomery Bird, Editor," *Pennsylvania Magazine of History and Biography,* LXXVI (April, 1952), 123-41. A study of Bird's political writing.

"Calavar," *Western Monthly Magazine* (Cincinnati), III (January, 1835), 41-49. One of the most interesting early reviews. Probably by James Hall.

CAMPBELL, KILLIS. "The Source of Poe's 'Some Words with a Mummy,'" *Nation,* XC (June 23, 1910), 625-26. Sees possible influence of Bird on Poe.

COWIE, ALEXANDER. *The Rise of the American Novel.* New York: American Book Company, 1948. The most thorough treatment of Bird and his contemporary novelists. Indispensable.

DURANG, CHARLES. "The Philadelphia Stage from the Year 1749 to the Year 1855," *Philadelphia Dispatch,* May 7, 1854; June 29, 1856; July 8, 1860. For Bird see particularly Series III, chapters 16 and 25. Very useful on the drama.

FISHER, SYDNEY GEORGE. "The Diaries of Sydney George Fisher 1837-1838," *Pennsylvania Magazine of History and Biography,* LXXVI (July, 1952), 330-52. Acid comments by a contemporary.

FOUST, CLEMENT E. *The Life and Dramatic Works of Robert Montgomery Bird.* New York: Knickerbocker Press, 1919. The standard life. Reprints *Pelopidas, The Gladiator, Oralloossa,* and *The Broker of Bogota.* Useful bibliography.

HARRIS, RICHARD. "From the Papers of R. M. Bird: The Last Scene from *News of the Night,*" University of Pennsylvania *Library*

Chronicle, XXIV (Winter, 1958), 1-12. Restores a lost scene to the early comedy.

————. "A Young Dramatist's Diary: *The Secret Records* of R. M. Bird," University of Pennsylvania *Library Chronicle*, XXV (Winter, 1959), 8-24. Bird's comments on his own dramatic career.

HUNT, THEODORE. *Le roman Américain, 1830-1850*. Paris: Libraire L. Rodstein, 1937. Good criticism though confused bibliography.

"An Itinerant Portrait Painter," University of Pennsylvania *Library Chronicle*, XIII (December, 1945), 99-133. Letters from the painter John Grimes to his close friend Bird.

KEISER, ALBERT. *The Indian in American Literature*. New York: Oxford University Press, 1933.

LEWIS, R. W. B. *The American Adam*. Chicago: University of Chicago Press, 1955. Includes a piquant analysis of Nathan Slaughter in relation to the theme of Adamism.

MOODY, RICHARD. *Edwin Forrest, First Star of the American Stage*. New York: Alfred A. Knopf, 1960. The most readable biography.

MOSES, MONTROSE J. *The American Dramatist*. Boston: Little, Brown and Co., 1911. Revised edition, 1925. Highly useful in any study of early American drama.

————. *The Fabulous Forrest*. Boston: Little, Brown and Co., 1929. See particularly Chapter V.

OBERHOLTZER, ELLIS PAXTON. *The Literary History of Philadelphia*. Philadelphia: George W. Jacobs, 1906. Useful for Bird's milieu and for comments on Bird.

PARRINGTON, VERNON LOUIS. *Main Currents in American Thought*. 3 vols. New York: Harcourt, Brace and Co., 1930. A few terse, stimulating comments.

Philadelphia *North American and United States Gazette*, January 24, 1854. Bird's obituary.

POE, EDGAR ALLAN. Reviews of *The Hawks of Hawk-Hollow* and *Sheppard Lee*. (Originally published in *Southern Literary Messenger*, II [December, 1835], 43-46; II [September, 1836], 662-67). Comment on Bird in "A Chapter on Autography." To be found in any complete edition of Poe's works. Always stimulating and intriguing though sometimes wrong-headed.

QUINN, ARTHUR HOBSON. *American Fiction, An Historical and Critical Survey*. New York: Appleton, Century Co., 1936.

————. "Dramatic Works of Robert Montgomery Bird." *Nation*, CIII (August 3, 1916), 108-9. Slight.

————. "The Establishment of National Literature." Part II of Quinn *et al.*, *The Literature of the American People*. New York:

Appleton, Century, Crofts, 1951. Includes a thorough, brief treatment of Bird.

————. *A History of the American Drama from the Beginning to the Civil War*. New York: Harper and Bros., 1923. Rev. ed., 1943. The pioneer and still standard work. Overlaudatory of Bird and other early dramatists but indispensable.

————. "Robert Montgomery Bird" in *Dictionary of American Biography*, II, 286-88.

REES, JAMES. *The Life of Edwin Forrest with Reminiscences and Personal Recollections*. Philadelphia: T. B. Peterson and Bros., 1874. On Bird, see particularly chapter 40. Exceedingly important as comment by an informed contemporary.

ROURKE, CONSTANCE M. *American Humor*. New York: Harcourt, Brace and Co., 1931. Reprinted by Anchor Books, 1955. Includes comment on Bird as "Western" humorist.

SCUDDER, HAROLD H. "Bartram's 'Travels': A Note on the Use of Bartram's 'Travels' by the Author of 'Nick of the Woods.'" *Notes and Queries*, CLXXXIV (March 13, 1943), 154-55.

SEILHAMMER, G. O. *History of the American Theatre*. 3 vols. Philadelphia, 1888-91.

SIMMS, WILLIAM GILMORE. *The Letters of William Gilmore Simms*. Eds. Mary C. Simms Oliphant, Alfred Taylor Odell, and T. C. Duncan Eaves. 5 vols. Columbia, S.C.: University of South Carolina Press, 1953. Correspondence with Bird.

THOMPSON, C. SEYMOUR, ed. "Travelling with Robert Montgomery Bird," University of Pennsylvania *Library Chronicle*, VII (March, 1939), 11-22, (June, 1939), 34-50, (October-December, 1939), 75-90; VIII (April, 1940), 4-21. Letters from Bird while he was traveling in the South, the West, and England.

VAN DOREN, CARL. "Fiction II: Contemporaries of Cooper." *Cambridge History of American Literature*. 3 vols. New York: G. P. Putnam's Sons, 1917. A good survey, including Bird.

WEMYSS, FRANCIS COURTNEY. *Twenty-six Years of the Life of an Actor and Manager*. 2 vols., New York: Burgess, Stringer and Co., 1847. Interesting light shed on Bird's plays by a contemporary actor.

WILLIAMS, CECIL B. "R. M. Bird's Plans for Novels of the Frontier," *American Literature*, XXI (November, 1949), 321-24. An important note commenting on several of Bird's numerous literary plans.

WILLIAMS, STANLEY T. *The Spanish Background of American Literature*. 2 vols. New Haven: Yale University Press, 1955. Remarks on the Spanish elements both in the novels of Mexico and in the two plays with South American settings.

Index